Professional ASP Programming Guide for Office Web Component

Professional ASP Programming Guide for Office Web Component

with Office 2000 and Office XP

Qimao Zhang

Writers Club Press
San Jose New York Lincoln Shanghai

**Professional ASP Programming Guide
for Office Web Component
with Office 2000 and Office XP**

Writers Club Press
an imprint of iUniverse.com, Inc.

For information address:
iUniverse.com, Inc.
5220 S 16th, Ste. 200
Lincoln, NE 68512
www.iuniverse.com

ISBN: 0-595-19846-5

Printed in the United States of America

"This book, like my heart and me, is dedicated to my wife Michelle L. Schafer. Without you, this will be impossible."

—Qimao Zhang

Contents

Chapter 0

Good Programming Practice

Establishing a good programming practice as early as possible is probably the most critical time-saving and headache-saving strategy. That is why this chapter is introduced ahead of all other chapters. The techniques discussed here are applicable to many programming environments and it comes from many professional programmers. Their advice is comes from their many years of learning and critical thinking throughout their programming careers. If you can use these techniques when you programme your projects, you will be more likely to produce robust, easily maintainable, and high-quality programs.

Write Self-Documenting Code

The first priority for programming is to establish a good programming practice. A good ASP page is always well designed and constructed. Several years ago, I reviewed some students' code from an introductory programming class. I found some code samples that looked like this:

```
Dim R, S, D, T
R = 40   S = 8   D = R*S*.05   T = R*S - D
```

Does this code work? Yes. Is this code easy to understand and maintain? No. This program lacks good programming style. The variables are uninformative and the layout is unclear. The same program can be written as follows:

```
Dim varHoursWorked, varHourlyRate, varInsurance, varSalary
    varHoursWorked = 40
    varHourlyRate = 8
    varInsurance = varHoursWorked * varHourlyRate * .05
    varSalary = varHoursWorked * varHourlyRate - varInsurance
```

The code section above is obviously used for salary calculation. It is much more readable and self-documenting:

- All variables are named well and used only for the purpose that they are used.
- All type names (var–variable) are descriptive enough to help data declarations.
- The program's layout corresponds to its logical structure.

You should establish some standard for naming conventions before you start programming. If the organization you work for already has some standards for naming conventions, you need to adopt it. Once you start programming, you should stick to the standard to be consistent. The standard should include the meanings for prefixes and abbreviations. For example, all text boxes starts with "txt", all list boxes starts with "lst", all strings starts with "str", all integers starts with "int", etc. Here is a general naming convention list for data types, you can create your own naming convention list, or you can follow other's naming convention list.

Table 0-1: Prefix Examples

Data Type	Prefix
Boolean	bln OR b
Byte	byt
Collection object	col
Currency	cur
Date-time	dtm
Double	dbl
Error	err
Integer	int OR i
Long	lng OR l
Object	obj OR o
String	str OR s
User-defined type	udt
Variant	vnt
ADO command	cmd
ADO connection	cnn OR c OR conn
ADO field	fld OR f
ADO parameter	prm
ADO recordset	rst OR rs

At a minimum, a useful naming convention will identify and distinguish variable type (object variable, control variable, and data type), variable scope, constants, and procedures, and it should be simple to understand and use. Microsoft has its naming convention list that adopted widely among many companies. For an example of a naming convention you can adopt or that you can use as the basis for your own convention, see MCS Naming Conventions.doc in the ODETools\V9\Samples\OPG\Appendixes folder on the Office 2000 Developer CD-ROM.

You should also avoid extremely long names even if they are meaningful. Try to be meaningful and concise. For example, "intMonthlyDisposableIncomePerHouseholdInCanada" is meaningful but too long. The name "MDC" is too short and not meaningful. The name "intMonIncomeCanada" is acceptable. You need to balance between meaningful and length to achieve the best combination of both.

You should also avoid using the name that maybe confusing with each other. For example, if you use "NumberRecords" and "RecordsNumber" at the same time, you will feel it is hard to keep track of their meanings and usage. It will be even more confusing for other people who read and maintain your code.

Always Use "Option Explicit"

The single most common reason for ASP programmers' frustration is the absence of the Option Explicit statement at the top of every ASP page. This requires you to declare a variable before using it in code. When it is not present, any variable found in your code will be assumed to be a valid variable—even a variable that you mistyped in a hurry. And that's where the problem lies: debugging a page that you know is correct but does not work properly. Can you see what's wrong with the following piece of code?

```
Dim varHoursWorked, varHourlyRate, varInsurance, varSalary
    varHoursWorked = 40
    varHourlyRatte = 8
    varInsurance = varHoursWorked * varHourlyRate * .05
    varSalary = varHoursWorked * varHourlyRate - varInsurance
```

Guess what is output from the above lines of code. You expected it to calculate the salary based on hourly rate of 8 dollars, but you get a results of ZERO. What happened?

There is a small typo. The third line of code instead of varHourlyRate = 8 it is varHourlyRatte = 8. A small mistake, but when the Option Explicit statement is not used, the ASP compiler that is chugging along interpreting/compiling your code stops in its tracks and says: "You need me to add the two values and place it in a brand new variable called varHourlyRatte. I will create a brand new variable for you." And that's what it does.

If you had placed the statement Option Explicit at the top of the above page, it would never complete its execution. This would give you a run time error "Variable undefined" pointing to the variable that is misspelled.

So get with the program! Always declare your variables before using them, and force this discipline by using the "Option Explicit" statement.

```
<% Option Explicit %>
```

The "Option Explicit" statement should be used for every ASP Page.

Provide Useful Comments

A useful comment is not a more verbose version of the code itself. A repetitious comment merely gives the reader more code to read without providing additional information. If your code is too complicated to understand, you need to improve your code first then add summary or intent comments.

A summary comment distills a few lines of code into one or two sentences. Users can scan them quickly without look into the code details. Summary comments are particularly useful when someone other than the code's original author tries to modify and maintain the code.

An intent comment explains the purpose of a section of code. Intent comment provide insights to understand original users' intent for that code section. Intent comment is usually useful during problem solving and debugging.

Effective commenting isn't that time-consuming. Too many comments are as bad as too few. You should develop a commenting style that easy to maintain and change. For example:

```
'  *********************************************
'  *    Author: David Smith                    *
'  *    Date: December 20th, 2002              *
'  *    *************************************
```

This comment looks pretty. But if you want to add another author, you have to move the * around to line it up nicely as original. Otherwise the comment section will looks like this:

```
'  *********************************************
'  *    Author: David Smith and Susan McDermott  *
'  *    Date: December 20th, 2002              *
'  *    *************************************
```

If you spend time fuss with the pretty column of asterisks on the both left and right, you are wasting your valuable time.

Another bad commenting style is end-line comments. For example:

```
Response.Write "<a href='result.asp?login='"
Response.Write strStatus & "'>Result</a>" 'status go to result.asp
```

End-line comments are hard to maintain. If the code line grows or shrinks, the end-line comment will move accordingly. The right side of coding area usually not very large, as you can see the example above, we have to truncate one line of code into two lines in order to fit the comment line. Therefore, many end-line comments tend to be cryptic.

A good comment should be efficient, clear, and not repeat the code. Most of the code paragraphs can be described into one-or two-sentence comments. The following comment is a good comment—it is easy to maintain and describes the code intent:

```
' check characters from InStr until last "\" found then
retrieve file name

varLen = Len(varFile)
iStart = varLen—1
While varFlag = 0
varFlag = InStr(iStart, varFile, "\")
        iStart = iStart—1
Wend

iStart = varLen—iStart—1
varFileFinal = Right(varFile, iStart)
```

Comments for variable declarations should describe aspects of variable that the variable can't describe. For example, if you have a number represents length of time, use comments to indicate if the unit is seconds, minutes, hours, months, or years.

You can also use comments to distinguish the difference between input and output data, why specific global or session variable is being used, in front of and after each control structure. Please keep each comment as close to the source as possible. Whenever the source code changes, you should change its comments accordingly. Otherwise, you will end up with some junk comments.

Robust Programming

A robust program should handling exceptions gracefully—"garbage in, error message out." While programming the code, you should always be prepared for exceptions. Your program should be able to gracefully handle the expected errors, and have a mechanism for handling the unexpected ones.

When getting data from users on the web page, check to be sure that the data falls in the allowable range. If there are many instances for same type of validation, you can put the validation code into a function. Then pass the original value into that function for validation check before using it. This way, you have built a firewall to insulate the errors into a special area for treatment. For example, before we can usea SQL string, we need to make sure the single quotes are being replaced before we retrieve recordset. Otherwise, we will have an error. We can use this function every time before we deploy a SQL string.

```
'_____

'Function name:sqlPrepare
'Purpose       :prepare SQL string for insertion into database
'Arguments     :string to be inserted, boolean indicating whether
               string
'Returns       :prepared string
'_____


   Function sqlPrepare(SQLExpr, IsString)

       Dim ReturnString

       If strIsEmpty(SQLExpr) Then
             sqlPrepare = "NULL"
       ElseIf IsString Then
             ReturnString = replace(SQLExpr, "'", "''")
             sqlPrepare = "'" & ReturnString & "'"
       Else
             sqlPrepare = SQLExpr
       End If

   End Function
```

Our program should also implement a mechanism for handling unexpected errors, the following code is used to trap unexpected errors and clear them:

```
On Error Resume Next
    'Place your program here

'Check for errors
If err.Number <> 0 Then
    'Write the error message
    Response.Write "Number: " & err.Number & "<p>"
    Response.Write "Description: " & err.Description & "<p>"
    Response.Write "Source: " & err.Source & "<p>"
    'clear the error
    err.clear
End If
```

You should always program against unexpected input and unexpected errors. With both validation and error handling, your program will be more robust.

Review before Release

In a perfect world, programmers will write perfect code that is bug free. Unfortunately, this is not a perfect world. We are blind to some of the trouble spots in our work, and other people may not have the same blind spots. That is why it's beneficial to have your code reviewed by somebody else before you release it. Of course, your own review is also very important and it should performed first.

The primary purpose of a technical review is to improve software quality. Some bugs appear when the user does not strictly follow the operation sequence, some bugs appear after an odd combination of inputs, some bugs appear after multiple runs of the same program. Therefore, code review will drastically reduce the number of bugs in your code.

Inspection is a special kind of code review that focus on inspect the areas that may have had problems in the past. Inspection usually takes much less time than testing so it is a time-saving technique. The emphasis on code review is early detection rather than correction. Before inspection, the author and reviewer should get together and go through the technical background of the code. Then the author and reviewer should come up with a list of areas that have been problems in the past, so the reviewer will inspect the code accordingly. For a large piece of code, multiple reviewers may need and each reviewer should have distinctive role to play.

Walkthrough is reading through the code and looking for errors. The purpose for walkthrough is to improve the technical quality of a program rather than assess it. The emphasis is on error detection, not correction. A walkthrough by other people will bring diverse viewpoints to the author. Walkthrough can also performed with a special focus such as finding logical errors.

Code reading usually involves two or more people reading the code independently. Code reading is an alternative to inspection and walkthroughs. In code reading, the reviewers will read the source code carefully and look for errors. Reviewers should also comment on the qualitative aspects of the code such as its design, style, readability, maintainability, and efficiency. Since code reading is performed independently, it can performed by reviewers from different locations. The author will consider the comments from all reviewers and make modifications or changes if necessary.

Unit testing is to test each unit thoroughly before you combine it with any other units. Therefore, you should do testing after every unit of code has been completed. It is usually much easier to find out the problem for a small unit of code than debug the whole program. A bug free unit has far better chance to integrate smoothly with other units. You should also test each function requirement to ensure your program has met the design specification.

Code Reuse and Efficiency

If you can reuse your previous code, you can save significant amount of coding time and increase productivity. In order for reuse, you can modularize parts of the program that you plan to reuse in other programs. For example, we can reuse the sqlPrepare function (shown in the Robust Programming section) in other programs to prepare SQL string. If you plan everything ahead of time, you should be able to reuse many modules you have built.

You can also analyze your current program to reuse some code within the program. If there is something in common from one place to another, the chance of reuse is possible. For example:

```
strSQLPA   =   "SELECT   employeeName,   employeeNumber,
employeeAddress, employeeCity, employeeState, employeeZip,
employeePhone, employeeEmail, employeeSSN, employeeSalary,
employeeDOB from Employee WHERE employeeState = 'PA'"
```

Then later on, you have another SQL string:

```
strSQLDC   =   "SELECT   employeeName,   employeeNumber,
employeeAddress, employeeCity, employeeState, employeeZip,
employeePhone, employeeEmail, employeeSSN, employeeSalary,
employeeDOB from Employee WHERE employeeCity = 'Washington'"
```

Finally, you have a SQL string looks like this:

```
strSQL = "SELECT employeeName, employeeNumber, employeeAddress,
employeeCity,   employeeState,   employeeZip,   employeePhone,
employeeEmail,   employeeSSN,   employeeSalary,   employeeDOB
from Employee ORDER BY employeeNumber"
```

The beginning part of these three strings is the same. So you can reuse part of the SQL string by using a temporary string to store the common characters:

```
strTemp   =   "SELECT   employeeName,   employeeNumber,
employeeAddress, employeeCity, employeeState, employeeZip,
employeePhone, employeeEmail, employeeSSN, employeeSalary,
employeeDOB from Employee WHERE "
strSQLPA = strTemp & "employeeState = 'PA'"
strSQLDC = strTemp & "employeeCity = 'Washington'"
strSQL = strTemp & "ORDER BY employeeNumber"
```

You can see nine lines of code condensed into six lines and the code is also cleaner. If you implement code reuse throughout your program, you will save a lot of time and effort. Many delayed projects can actually to be delivered on time if the programmers know how to reuse their code. Therefore, design your code efficiently and plan ahead.

Site navigation and banner graphics should be handled using include files. By doing so, developers will simply be able to reference a single-source for all navigational elements.

The include files themselves will have programming logic embedded that will dynamically decide which navigational elements to show, banners to include, rollovers to offer, ETC. While this will cause some additional overhead when generating pages, the time saved by not updating individual pages or maintaining several navigation modules will be extremely beneficial.

Further, developers responsible for site look and feel can update navigational elements and site graphics globally. Individual developers creating other modules will be able to focus on the task at hand without worrying about navigational elements. When the navigational elements need to be changed, a developer can change them on one file then all the navigation layout will be modified at the same time. Otherwise, the developer has to change every page for the same navigation modification.

All include files that include server-side code should use the ".asp" extension to prevent potential downloading of files. The ".asp" extension interprets any code prior to sending it to the client, thereby making it more difficult for the end user to download sensitive code.

To include files, use the following syntax:

➤ If the include file is located in the subfolder at same level:

```
<!--#INCLUDE FILE="/includes/header.asp"-->
```

➤ If the include file is located in the different folder at different level:

```
<!--#INCLUDE FILE="../../../../includes/header.asp"-->
```

➤ If the include file is located in the same folder:

```
<!--#INCLUDE FILE="header.asp"-->
```

➤ If you want to include the file always in the same folder then you can use include virtual:

```
<!--#INCLUDE Virtual="includes/header.asp"-->
```

For the great benefits mentioned above, it is a great idea to put header into a .asp file, left navigation into a .asp file, footer into a .asp file. Then on every page, just include header file on the top, left file on the left, and footer file on the bottom. Then you can focus on programming without worrying about the details of navigation and layout.

Summary

We use the chapter 0 means the materials covered in this chapter is not directly about Office Web Components. But the reason we put it here is for strategic reasons: before you starting coding Office Web Components, establishing a good programming norm is the key to success.

You can also add more insights to this section from your own experience and gradually develop your own programming styles. A good computing professional is usually eager to learn from any resource at anytime. The resource could be a book, your own mistake, a co-worker's documentation, a web site, etc. These efforts will pay off handsome rewards to your projects and your career.

Since this book is about ASP, we will use ASP as our examples for all topics. The code samples are used for illustration purpose only, you are not expected to understand how it works at this point.

You should also realize, if the company or client you are working for has its own standards regarding to programming styles, you should follow those standards.

Chapter 1

Introduction to Office Web Components

This chapter will introduce the Office Web Components. The Office Web Components are a collection of Microsoft Component Object Model (COM) controls designed to make it possible for you publish fully interactive worksheets, charts, PivotTable reports, and databases to the Web. When users view a Web page that contains an Office Web Component, they can interact with the data displayed right in Microsoft Internet Explorer. Users can sort, filter, add, or change data, expand and collapse detail views, work with PivotTable lists, and chart the results of their changes. In addition, the Office Web Components are fully programmable, which makes it possible for you create rich, interactive content for Web-based applications.

Installation

The Microsoft Office Web Components (OWC) comes with Office 2000 and Office XP CD. If you do not have the OWC installed, you may install it from those CDs onto your web server. To view and work with any of the Office Web Components, users must either have Office 2000 or Office XP installed, or if your company has an Office 2000 or Office XP site license, they must download the Office Web Components from your corporate intranet. Please see *What's New in Office XP OWC* section in this chapter for more details regarding Office XP OWC installation and configuration.

Please note The Office Web Components work only in Internet Explorer 4.01 or later. Office Web Components on Microsoft Access data access pages work only in Internet Explorer 5 or later. In addition, you get the most complete functionality with all of the Office Web Component controls in Internet Explorer 5 or later.

Types of OWC Components

There are four types of OWC Components: Chart Component, PivotTable Component, Spreadsheet Component, and Data Source Component. Table 1.1 shows the OWC Components, their COM control, Object, and description.

Table 1.1: OWC Components

Office Web Component	COM control	Object	Description
Spreadsheet Component	Spreadsheet	Spreadsheet	This component provides a recalculation engine, a full function library, and a simple worksheet user interface for use on Web pages.
Chart Component	Chart	Chart Space	This component displays a graphical representation of data from a Spreadsheet, PivotTable List, or Data Source component. When bound to other controls on a page, the Chart component updates instantly in response to changes made to the bound controls.
PivotTable Component	PivotTable List	PivotTable	This component makes it possible for users to sort, group, filter, outline, and manipulate data from a worksheet, database, or multidimensional data cube.
Data Source Component	Data Source	DataSource Control	This control manages communication between a Web page or controls on the page and the source of data for the page. This control provides the reporting engine behind data access pages as well as the PivotTable List control.

The Chart Component

The Chart component is a COM control that makes it possible for you create a two-dimensional graphical representation of data displayed in a Web page in Microsoft Internet Explorer 4.01 or later. You get the most complete functionality with this control, and all of the Office Web Component controls, by using Internet Explorer 5 or later. You can create three-dimensional graphics in Office XP version of Chart Component.

The Chart component can be bound to a Spreadsheet component, a Data Source component, a PivotTable List control, an ADO recordset, or any COM control that supports data binding. You can bind the chart to a local data source (data stored in the HTML code in the page itself) or to a remote data source (data stored in a Microsoft Access or Microsoft SQL Server™ database, for example). As data changes in the data source, the Chart component automatically updates, scales, and sizes itself appropriately.

You can insert a Chart component in a Web page in several ways:

➤ In Microsoft Excel, you can add a Chart component to a Web page by using the Chart wizard to create a chart and then using the Publish as Web Page dialog box to create a Web page that contains the chart.

➤ In Access, you can add a chart to a data access page by clicking the Office Chart tool in the toolbox and then clicking the place on the page where you want the chart to appear. Double clicking the chart space in the data access page displays a dialog, which steps you through the process of connecting the chart to a data source.

➤ In Microsoft FrontPage, you can add a Chart component to a page by pointing to Component on the Insert menu, and then clicking Office Chart. This inserts an empty Chart component on the page, but unlike in Access, the Office Chart wizard is not launched. To bind the control to data, you use Microsoft Visual Basic Scripting Edition (VBScript) code in the Web page.

In addition, you can insert a Chart component directly in a Web page by adding an <OBJECT> tag for the control to the page and specifying the control's CLSID as the setting for the CLASSID attribute. Then, you can use Visual Basic for Applications (VBA) or VBScript code to work with the chart programmatically.

In Chapter 2 and Chapter 3, we will cover how to program each different type of chart programmatically. Figure 1.1 shows an example of a Chart component:

Figure 1.1 Column Chart: Number of New Customers

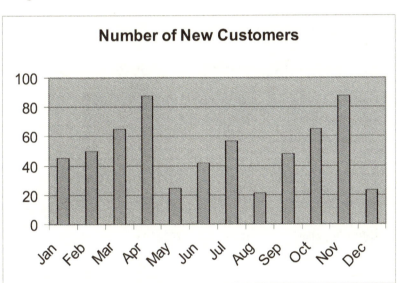

The CLSID for the Chart component and all the objects and related methods and properties for the control are documented in the owcvba10.chm Help file.

Note

The path to the owcvba10.chm Help file reflects the language ID folder (1033) for U.S. English language support in Office. The language ID folder c:\program files\common files\microsoft shared\web components\10\<langid>differs for each language.

The Spreadsheet Component

The Spreadsheet component is a Microsoft COM control that makes it possible for you to add the functionality of a worksheet to a Web page. You can also place a hidden instance of this control on a page and use it as a powerful recalculation engine that works with other visible controls on a page. You can think of this control as a way to take the power behind an Excel worksheet and transfer it to a Web page.

You can think of the Spreadsheet component as a miniature version of an Excel spreadsheet. You can recalculate values; sort, filter, and scroll data; protect cells; and even reload the data back to Excel 2000 or Excel XP for further data analysis, etc.

Figure 2.2 Spreadsheet Component Example

	A	B	C	D	E
1	**Utility Expenses**	**Jan**	**Feb**	**Mar**	**Apr**
2	Water	2563.23	3562.12	3658.21	4012.56
3	Electric	7852.12	6206.45	5523.42	4858.79
4	Gas	11456.85	8956.23	7745.12	6021.11
5					
6	**Total**	21872.2	18724.8	16926.75	14892.46
7					
8	**Office Supplies**	6032.22	7832.71	6306.52	7614.89
9					
10	Total	6032.22	7832.71	6306.52	7614.89
11					
12					
13					
14					
15					
16					
17					
18					
19					

The PivotTable Component

The PivotTable Component provides interactive data reporting and analysis. Using the PivotTable component, you can view, sort, group, and calculate data in many different ways. You can also create dynamic reports based on live data.

If you are creating a PivotTable list from a relational data source, the PivotTable Service is used to create a multidimensional data cube from the relational data bound to the Data Source component. This data cube is used by the PivotTable component. For multidimensional data sources, the PivotTable component relies upon an OLE DB for online analytical processing (OLAP) provider. The PivotTable Service is the OLE DB for OLAP provider for Microsoft SQL Server OLAP Services.

For example, Figure 2.3 is a time-off tracking system for employees in the department. You can select any employee or all employees, any type of time-off or all types, any month or all months, then the PivotTable component will automatically calculate and display the data based on your selection.

Figure 2.3 Time-Off Tracking Pivot Table

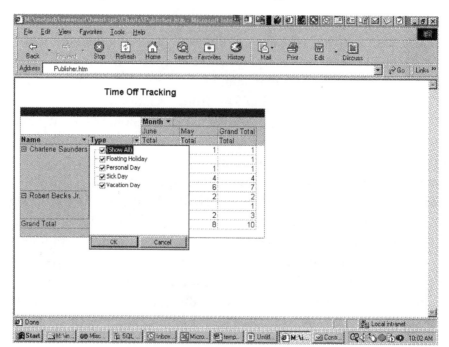

The Data Source Component

The Data Source component is best understood as the reporting engine behind data access pages, PivotTable List controls, and data-bound Chart components. The Data Source component has no visual representation. It is designed to manage the connection to the underlying data source and deliver records to be displayed by other controls on a Web page.

The Data Source component relies on ADO for connections to relational data sources such as Microsoft Access, Microsoft SQL Server™, or Oracle databases. Although the Data Source component can provide data to the PivotTable List control, the Data Source component cannot be bound to multidimensional data sources; transformations of relational data to multidimensional data are managed by the PivotTable Service.

You can use the Data Source component to do the following:

➤ Associate a DataSourceControl object with a database connection.

➤ Add a record (row) source (table, view, stored procedure, or SQL statement) to a Data Source component.

➤ Provide an ADO recordset to data-consuming objects on a Web page. These objects include the Microsoft Internet Explorer built-in controls that can be data bound, such as the TEXT or SELECT control, and all of the other Office Web Component controls.

➤ Build SQL commands to request data from relational data sources.

➤ Construct hierarchical (shaped) Recordset objects from one or more data providers by using the services of the Microsoft Data Shaping Service for OLE DB service provider.

➤ Persist data in an Office Web Component to a file or load data from a file to an Office Web Component.

Note

Although you can work directly with the Data Source component, in many cases you are not required to. For example, when you create an Access data access page and add fields to the page by dragging them from the field list, Access automatically adds a properly configured Data Source component to the page.

What's New in Office XP OWC

The Office XP Web Components (OWC) has many new features and improvements over the great set of features that shipped in Office 2000. If you will upgrade from Office 2000 to Office XP, please take some time to read this document and see how the changes to the OWC will affect your applications.

Programming Model Changes

The Spreadsheet Component has been improved quite significantly to be more compatible with Excel. This involves changing substantial parts of its object model to be fully compatible with Excel.

Moreover, it also supports workbooks with multiple sheets which is a fundamental architecture change.

The Chart and PivotTable Components have not changed radically in terms of object model changes from Office 2000. However, in the course of improving the feature sets of these components, some old object model members have been removed.

Some changes include:

➢ Chart's databinding model has been simplified.

➢ Binding a chart to a PivotTable list has also been changed and is much easier now. The PivotTable Component version 2000's filter object model has been removed in favor of a much more robust object model in version 2002 (there are a lot more filtering features in version 2002, such as top N filtering as well as multiple filters on the filter axis).

➢ When changing data sources for the PivotTable list, DataMember is no longer automatically cleared.

➢ Also, the XMLData blobs that the chart and PivotTable list in version 2000 emit–often used in solutions to 'save' the current PivotTable list or chart as a report–is forward compatible with their version 2002 counterparts.

New Filenames and Interface Ids

Office XP introduces the second version of the Office Web Components. To allow for side by side use with the Office 2000 version, the DLLs have been renamed and new GUIDs generated for all of the interfaces.

> **New Names and GUIDs**
>
> All of the file names will include the new version number (10). For example **msowc.dll** will become **owc10.dll** (see below for more details). All of the GUIDs have been moved to new values in the assigned range.

> **Shipping Office 2000 Controls in Office XP**
>
> Office 2000 controls (latest SR level) are shipped in Office XP and installed into the same location as they are currently. For upgrades from Office 2000 to Office XP this will not require any action. For installations on machines without Office 2000 both sets of controls will be installed.

> **Persistence Compatibility**
>
> Office XP controls will read the persistence of the Office 2000 controls (XML data). The Office 2000 controls will not be able to read the persistence of the Office XP controls.

> **New File Names**
>
> The 'MS' prefix is dropped; the two extra letters are instead used for the version number. This maintains the current 8.3 file names and a consistent prefix (OWC).

Table 1.2 Old and New file names

Old Name	New Name	Note
MSOWC.DLL	OWC10.DLL	Main control DLL
MSOWCF.DLL	<Not in v10>	WebCalc function library
MSOWCINI.DLL	<Not in v10>	Web Install localized resources
MSOWC.SLL	<Not in v10>	Toolbox
MSOWCI.DLL	OWCI10.DLL	Main localized resources
MSOWCW.DLL	<Not in v10>	Wizard
MSOWCWI.DLL	<Not in v10>	Wizard localized resources
MSOWCRPL.CHM	OWCRPL10.CHM	Help file
MSOWCRDP.CHM	OWCRDP10.CHM	Help file
MSOWCRSS.CHM	OWCRSS10.CHM	Help file
MSOWCDSS.CHM	OWCDSS10.CHM	Help file
MSOWCDPL.CHM	OWCDPL10.CHM	Help file
MSOWCVBA.CHM	OWCVBA10.CHM	Help file
MSOWCDCH.CHM	OWCDCH10.CHM	Help file
MSOWCFUN.CHM	OWCFUN10.CHM	Help file
<new>	OWCRCH10.CHM	Help file

New Setup and Install Locations

The Office Web Components (OWC) will be installed using owc10.msi and setup.exe only. A local version of Office's setup.exe is copied to the root directory in the setup image. The action for setup.exe is customized using a local setup.ini file.

> ➤ Use of ALT HTML
>
> Applications that publish web pages containing the Office Web Components can insert <alt html> into the <object> tag that provides a user instructions and a link to a setup.exe.

➤ Dropping Codebase

Support for using the codebase attribute of the <object> tag has been discontinued as the Component Download Service does not provide the support needed to do an install. Files published with OWC should not contain a codebase. A side effect of this is that it is not possible for a page to automatically upgrade the OWC from an older version (that is from RTM to SR1)

(note—this does not effect v2000 to v2002 upgrades).

➤ Location of Setup.exe and owc10.msi

The setup.exe program for the OWC (which is not the setup.exe for Office) is located in the files/owc directory (at all times).

Table 1.3: Set up file locations

Situation	File Locations
CD	owc10.msi is located in the CD root\setup.exe is located in \files\owc OWC files are located in \office10.cab
Office setup image (setup.exe /a)	owc10.msi is located in the setup root\setup.exe is located in \files\owc OWC files are located in \files\...
OWC setup image (files\owc\setup.exe /a)	owc10.msi is located in the setup root\setup.exe is located in \files\owc OWC files are located in \files\...

➤ **Creating an Admin Image**

An OWC only setup image can be created in two easy steps:

a) Run **msiexec.exe /a owc.msi** from a command prompt (it will present an UI that lets you choose your admin install location).

b) Copy all files from **<CD root>\files\osp\<lcid>** to **<admin-image-root>\files\osp\<lcid>**. This will provide the Office System Pack.

Installed Files and Locations

The components will be installed into **\Program Files\Common Files\Microsoft Shared\Web Components\10** (referenced as **\<root\>** below). Locale files will be installed into numbered locale directories below **\<root\>** (that is, international resource DLLs are installed into **\<root\>\\<locale\>**). References to **\<oledb\>** indicate **\Program files\Common files\System\OLE DB**

Table 1.4: Installed files and locations

File	Location	Note
OWC Core Files		
Owc10.dll	\<root\>	Main control DLL
owci10.dll	\<root\>\\<locale\>	Main localized resources
owcrpl10.chm	\<root\>\\<locale\>	Help file (PivotTable runtime)
owcrdp10.chm	\<root\>\\<locale\>	Help file (Datapages runtime)
owcrss10.chm	\<root\>\\<locale\>	Help file (Spreadsheet runtime)
owcfun10.chm	\<root\>\\<locale\>	Help file (Function library)
owcrch10.chm	\<root\>\\<locale\>	Help file (Chart runtime)
Client Data Manager		
mscdm.dll	...\Microsoft Shared\MSClientDataMgr	
D3D for NT4		
dd7nt4.dll	\<root\>	Software only Direct Draw
d3d7nt4.dll	\<root\>	Renamed D3D IM

Visual Studio 7 Runtime		
msvcr70.dll	\Program Files\ Microsoft Office\ Office10\VS Runtime	C runtime
msvcp70.dll	\Program Files\ Microsoft Office\ Office10\VS Runtime	C++ runtime
vswin9x.dll	\Program Files\ Microsoft Office\ Office10\VS Runtime	C runtime for Win9x clients
System Files		
ucs20.dll	...\Microsoft Shared\ Office10\	BiDi support
Usp10.dll	...\Microsoft Shared\ Office10\	BiDi Support
Mscomctl.ocx	\<system32\>	Common Control OCX
PivotTable Services 8.0		
msolap80.dll	\<oledb\>	
msolap80.rll	\<oledb\>\resources\<locale\>	
Msdmeng.dll	\<oledb\>	
msdmine.dll	\<oledb\>	
msdmine.rll	\<oledb\>\resources\<locale\>	
msmdun80.dll	\<oledb\>	
msmdcb80.dll	\<oledb\>	
msmdgd80.dll	\<oledb\>	
msolui80.dll	\<oledb\>	
olapuir.rll	\<oledb\>\resources\<locale\>	

New Licensing Overview

The Office Web Components (OWC) can now be distributed without an Office license. The OWC run in a View Only mode when there is no Office license on the machine.

The OWC supports the new license files of Office XP. For the OWC to be interactive an Office XP license file must be present on the host machine. If a license is not present then the OWC will support a 'View Only mode' which allows users to see the content of the controls but not manipulate it.

The OWC supports License Package File (LPK) licensing in addition to Office license files. Placing an LPK license file on a web server will enable interactive content. The use of LPK license files is restricted to instances when it can be assured that every client that views a web page containing the OWC has a valid Office license (that is, through an Enterprise Agreement).

➤ **Design-time Requires an Office License**

Use of the OWC in Design Mode (in FrontPage, VID, VB, etc) requires an Office license which only gets installed by Office products. Components will not instantiate in design mode if the license is not on the machine or passed in by the host application. An Office license is required to create or edit content with the OWC.

➤ **Interactive Runtime Requires an Office License**

The OWC will only operate in interactive mode if an Office license is on the machine or is passed in by the host application. If the license validation fails, the components will operate in static view-only mode.

➤ **Static Runtime Use is Free**

Static runtime is free and will be enforced by a license check. Static runtime use of the components or static content generated by the Office Components is allowed without an Office license. All forms of runtime use of the **Data Source component** is allowed without an Office license.

➤ **Office Web Components Licensing Implementation**

The OWC uses a two-step licensing check that combines standard COM control licensing with the new Office licensing. The existence of a control license takes precedence over an Office license. The OWC will check for view-only mode with the following logic:

```
if ( ValidControlLicense() )
{
    InteractiveMode()
}
else if ( ValidOfficeLicense() )
{
    InteractiveMode()
}
else
{
    ViewOnlyMode()
}
```

The OWC can receive a control license through the **CoCreateInstanceLic** interface either from an Microsoft application or from Microsoft Internet Explorer via an LPK file.

Chart Component

➤ **3D charts add depth to your data**: The Chart Component has been added for a number of 3D chart types including Column, Bar, Pie and Area. Approximately 30% of all column, bar, and pie charts use 3D for visual effect. Using DirectX, rich modeled 3D charts will add pizzazz to presentations.

➤ **Built in datasheet**: You can now use a datasheet to enter static data for your chart. Although it is very powerful to create data-bound charts that automatically update as the underlying data changes, a large percentage of charts consist of very few data points, based on static data.

➤ **Simplified data binding**: By integrating the data binding support in the PivotTable Component, the Chart Component will now support binding directly to a data source, along with sorting, grouping, and filtering of the data. This, along with new control level properties, will let authors create a chart using only the property toolbox.

➤ **Fill effects**: The chart authors can now create richer charts using gradient fill-effects, textures, and images. Using the Office Art library, chart can now support the same Office fill effects used by Graph.

➤ **Pivot your chart**: The PivotTable list has adopted (and make improvements on) the Excel pivot UI. The Chart Component uses a similar convention for supporting PivotCharts. Support includes chart drag/drop, drop areas, drilling into a data point like a bar or pie slice, field list as drag source, and multi-plot.

➤ **Toolbar for quick modifications**: The chart will now provide more direct interaction in runtime and design time with a toolbar to give users quick and easy access to frequent commands.

➤ **Improved chart wizard**: The improved chart wizard will be integrated into the new property toolbox with simplified steps, better data binding support, and reentrancy. Making the chart wizard functionality completely re-entrant by integrating it into the toolbox allows users to make the changes they need, and when they need to, without losing any work.

➤ **Time scale axis**: A recent survey of real-world charts have shown that well over 50% of all column, line, and area charts use dates and time in their chart. With added special handling for date/time data, the chart will fill in missing dates, sort dates in the correct order, group data points by time intervals, and present a visually appealing axis that is intelligent about labels, tick-marks, and gridline intervals.

➤ **Custom drawing events and methods**: The Chart Component exposes drawing events and methods that allow custom chart visuals such as additional labeling, markers, or even whole new chart types. This lets developers create the custom solutions needed by high-end customers.

➤ **Use layers to display two series each with different scaling**: To give users better control over how series are rendered and scaled, methods are added to the chart to make it possible to create a line chart with two series each having a different scaling.

➤ **Improved axis labels**: The chart will improve its display of category axis labels with better layout and more user options such as label rotation.

➤ **Passive alerts**: Now when a non-critical error occurs, users will see a small icon in the chart that they can click to get more details.

➤ **Conditional formatting (format maps)**: This allows users to associate ranges of values with formatting such as ranges of color and other format settings.

PivotTable Components

➢ **Improved filtering with support for top and bottom N filters**: Now you can create conditional filters for a richer slice of your data. Create filters to show the top or bottom 10 items based on count, sum, or percent.

➢ **Calculated totals and detail fields**: Authors can extend the information presented to users by creating new fields and totals using expressions. Calculated detail fields like "Price*Quantity" can be added to the PivotTable list as well as new calculated totals for analysis like "Budget/Actual" or growth from the same period last year.

➢ **New AutoCalc functions**: When working with relational data, there is support for the new AutoCalc functions for average, standard deviation, and variance.

➢ **Select multiple items in filter fields**: Now you can select more than one item to filter when a field is in the filter area. By doing so, you will see the aggregate of the selected items in the report.

➢ **Grouping intervals**: Developers or end users can group detail field values into higher-level buckets: by their first one or two letters, by every 10 if it is a numeric field, or by date/time intervals.

➢ **Display your totals as a percentage**: Now you can analyze your information by comparing percentages across a row or column. Values can be displayed as a percentage of row, column, grand or row/column parent total.

➢ **Support for unbalanced and ragged hierarchies**: Microsoft OLAP Services and the OLE DB for OLAP spec are defining support for unbalanced and ragged hierarchies. The PivotTable Component will support these new types of hierarchies.

➤ **Custom ordering of members**: In many reporting situations, users require explicit control over the ordering of members on an axis. Now you can order members exactly the way you want them. Just select a member and drag it where you want it.

➤ **Ad-hoc member grouping**: Users will be able to group members together with a combined total in a new level. For example, now you can group the sales folks that report to you into a custom group with appropriate totals.

➤ **Display member properties**: If information has been associated with a member, the PivotTable Component will display it to users. For example, a store might have additional information associated with it like a phone number, the name of the manager, and hours of operation. Cube designers use member properties for information that is related to a member, but should not be used to create additional levels of aggregation. Member properties can also contain statistics produced by the data mining features being built into SQL Server 2000 Analysis Services.

➤ **New options for drilling into your data**: Drilling down a hierarchy to automatically add the next level is now supported.

➤ **Updatability**: One of the key features in this release is support in detail data for updating, inserting, and deleting data. This is essential when the PivotTable Component is used as a sublist in Data Access Pages or when it is used to edit a simple list of data.

➤ **Hyperlink support**: Now authors will have built-in support for hyperlinks just like the Spreadsheet Component. When clicked, the hyperlink navigates the current window to the specified URL in the hyperlink. Hyperlinks fields can be specified by the author or in the case of Jet or SQL Server tables, they are automatically recognized and enabled.

➤ **More ways to load data**: Now the PivotTable Component can load and offer full functionality against a wider variety of data sources including ADO Recordsets, any Data Source component (custom or otherwise), or an XML-Rowset stream.

➤ **Friendlier error information**: The PivotTable Component will display richer error information in response to a query or connection failure. If the component is unbound, better feedback or error information is given and an easy way to bind the control is offered.

➤ **Use custom MDX to display a pivot**: With support for custom MDX, developers can handcraft complex Multidimensional Expressions (MDX) and make the PivotTable component use that for its initial query to the OLAP source.

➤ **Support for time levels in AutoDate hierarchies**: Hours, Minutes, and Seconds levels are added to the AutoDate hierarchies generated if the underlying field has a time portion.

➤ **Bind to data using a multi-dimensional Connection object**: Now you can hand the PivotTable Component an existing connection. This allows developers to modify provider-specific settings on the Connection object before handing it to the component. One can also access the current session used by the control to execute specific statements on the same session.

➤ **Track Recordset currency while pivoted**: The currency indicator is now visible while grouped and the currency arrow tracks currency changes across child Recordsets.

Spreadsheet

➤ **Calculation engine**: The Spreadsheet features a new calculation component that is able to provide greater performance, robustness, and compatibility with Excel. The new calculation component was built from Excel's source code to provide the highest level of compatibility and dependability. By building this component from Excel's sources, all of Excel's built-in formulas, perfect dependencies, array formulas, and discontinuous references are supported.

➤ **Names**: Names are an important feature for the Calculation engine that allows users to define a name for a range of cells, a constant, and functions. The name can then be used in formulas. Names are interchangeable with Excel.

➤ **IDispatch as a new, in-cell data type**: The list of built-in data types has been expanded to include IDispatch. Numbers, text, booleans, dates, errors, arrays and IDispatch are now supported. These allow savvy model builders to reference properties of COM objects (for example, MSXML) using a formula-like syntax.

➤ **Container formulas**: Providing IDispatch as a new, intrinsic data type to a spreadsheet's cells enables formulas to be easily added which allows the users to data-bind cells to elements from the container. This allows a Web-based solution using the Spreadsheet component to data-bind to HTML elements such as text boxes, list boxes, or even textual elements.

➤ **Support for XML-Spreadsheet**: Both Excel and the Spreadsheet Component will share a common file format that will make it easy for customers to construct, process, share, and extract data from their spreadsheet models. The Spreadsheet Component supports load/save, copy/paste, and Range.Value with XML-Spreadsheet.

➤ **Workbooks**: Just like classic Excel, Spreadsheet users can now work with a collection of sheets in a workbook. This helps users organize their information. By keeping related sheets in the same workbook, it is easier for users to make related changes and edits, to consolidate related sheets, or to do calculations involving data from multiple worksheets. This will also provide better fidelity when publishing from or exporting to Excel. Excel will be adding the option to publish a workbook with interactivity.

> **Excel-compatible object model**: The Spreadsheet's object model has been re-implemented to be source code compatible with Excel for all of the functionality that is supported. This means that for all of the functionality provided by the Spreadsheet Component, Excel's properties, methods, and events naming conventions are used. In some cases, the full functionality of an Excel method could not be supported (for example, password protection is not supported) but the object model syntax is identical to Excel. This will make it easier for Excel VBA developers to build solutions against the Spreadsheet, and also ease the process of moving solutions from Office XP Spreadsheet solutions to the next generation of Office.

> **Data-bound sheets**: The Spreadsheet Component now has an intrinsic way to connect to data stored in databases like SQL Server. A data-bound sheet gets its data from a table or view in a database and can be refreshed by the user. The size of the sheet is determined by the amount of data in the database and named ranges are automatically created to help users build formulas against data-bound data.

> **More rows and columns**: The Spreadsheet Component now supports 262,144 rows by 18,278 columns.

> **Custom row and column headers**: This enables developers to customize the text that is displayed in the row and column headers through scripting. Custom text headings allow the Chart Component to use the Spreadsheet Component as their datasheet.

> **New look-and-feel**: The Spreadsheet Component has been updated to look like the rest of Office XP with the addition of lightened row and column headings with highlights to help indicate the active selection.

Summary

In this chapter, we briefly looked at the Office Web Components. There are four types of OWC components: Chart component, Spreadsheet component, PivotTable component, and Data Source component.

We also looked at the installation issues and what's new in Office XP OWC. Office XP OWC has added and improved many functions to Office 2000.

The next chapter we will introduce Chart component and chart types. Chart component is a widely used component to display data in graphical format on the web site.

Chapter 2

Introduction to Chart Component

Among all OWC components, the Chart component is considered as the most widely used component for business applications. Basically, a chart presents a table of numbers visually. Displaying data in a well-conceived chart can make the data more understandable, and you often can make your point more quickly as a result. Because a chart presents a picture, charts are particularly useful for understanding a lengthy series of numbers and their relationships. Making a chart helps you to spot trends and patterns that would be nearly impossible to identify when examining a range of numbers. Chart component is also considered as the most difficult type of OWC component for programming due to its complexity. Therefore, we designated three chapters to cover Chart component.

Chart Types

OWC supports many types of charts correspond to Excel chart types: bar charts, pie chart, line chart, area chart, stock chart, etc. Even some exotic chart types are supported, such as polar chart, radar chart, etc. Table 2.1 lists OWC chart types and the constants associated with them.

Table 2.1: Chart Types for Office Web Components

Chart Type	Description	Constant	Value
Combination	Combination chart	chChartTypeCombo	-1
Column	Clustered Column	chChartTypeColumnClustered	0
	Stacked Column	chChartTypeColumnStacked	1
	100% Stacked Column	chChartTypeColumnStacked100	2
Bar	Clustered Bar	chChartTypeBarClustered	3
	Stacked Bar	chChartTypeBarStacked	4
	100% Stacked Bar	chChartTypeBarStacked100	5
Line	Line	chChartTypeLine	6
	Line with Markers	chChartTypeLineMarkers	7
	Stacked Line	chChartTypeLineStacked	8
	Stacked Line with Markers	chChartTypeLineStackedMarkers	9
	100% Stacked Line	chChartTypeLineStacked100	10
	100% Stacked Line with Markers	chChartTypeLineStacked100Markers	11
	Smooth Line	chChartTypeSmoothLine	12
	Smooth Line with Markers	chChartTypeSmoothLineMarkers	13
	Smooth Stacked Line	chChartTypeSmoothLineStacked	14
	Smooth Stacked Line with Markers	chChartTypeSmoothLineStackedMarkers	15
	Smooth 100% Stacked Line	chChartTypeSmoothLineStacked100	16
	Smooth 100% Stacked Line with Markers	chChartTypeSmoothLineStacked100Markers	17
Pie	Pie	chChartTypePie	18
	Exploded Pie	chChartTypePieExploded	19
	Stacked Pie	chChartTypePieStacked	20
XY Scatter	Scatter	chChartTypeScatterMarkers	21
	Scatter with Smoothed Lines and Markers	chChartTypeScatterSmoothLineMarkers	22
	Scatter with Smoothed Lines and No Markers	chChartTypeScatterSmoothLine	23
	Scatter with Lines and Markers	chChartTypeScatterLineMarkers	24
	Scatter with Lines and No Markers	chChartTypeScatterLine	25
	Scatter with Filled Lines	chChartTypeScatterLineFilled	26
Bubble	Bubble	chChartTypeBubble	27
	Bubble with Line	chChartTypeBubbleLine	28
Area	Area	chChartTypeArea	29
	Stacked Area	chChartTypeAreaStacked	30
	100% Stacked Area	chChartTypeAreaStacked100	31
Doughnut	Doughnut	chChartTypeDoughnut	32
	Exploded Doughnut	chChartTypeDoughnutExploded	33
Radar	Radar	chChartTypeRadarLine	34
	Radar with Data Markers	chChartTypeRadarLineMarkers	35
	Filled Radar	chChartTypeRadarLineFilled	36
	Radar with Smooth Line	chChartTypeRadarSmoothLine	37
	Radar with Smooth Line and Data Markers	chChartTypeRadarSmoothLineMarkers	38
Stock	Volume-High-Low-Close	chChartTypeStockHLC	39
	Volume-Open-High-Low-Close	chChartTypeStockOHLC	40
Polar	Polar with Markers	chChartTypePolarMarkers	41
	Polar with Lines	chChartTypePolarLine	42
	Polar with Lines and Markers	chChartTypePolarLineMarkers	43
	Polar with Smooth Lines	chChartTypePolarSmoothLine	44
	Polar with Smooth Lines and Markers	chChartTypePolarSmoothLineMarkers	45

A commonly asked question regarding to charting is which chart type is appropriate for the data. Although this question may looks simple at the first glance, it is not easy to develop any hard-and-fast rules for determining which chart type is best of your data. The bottom line is to use the chart type that gets your message across in the simplest way.

The column chart is probably the best choice for discrete units for each interval. For example, the number of new customers for local customer service center:

Figure 2.1 Column Chart: Number of New Customers

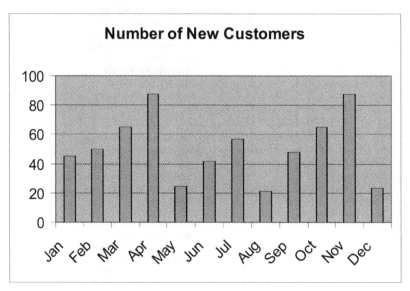

A line chart or area chart for the above data will not be appropriate. Because line chart and area chart are best for continuous data and they show trend of change between intervals. For example, a water leakage from a boiler will be better represented in a area chart or line chart:

Figure 2.2 Area Chart: Water Leakage in the Boiler

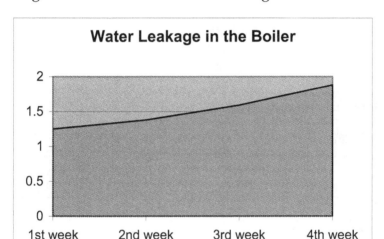

We will discuss more of the characteristics of some chart types in the charting sections. To better understand the visual display of quantitative information, data analysis and create visually arresting charts, you can pick up a book in the area of statistical evidence and information design.

Chart Elements

All charts composed of elements. Understand the chart elements is the first step to understand the chart and modify the characteristics of the chart. Figure xx.1 shows the hierarchy of chart elements in a chart space.

Figure 2.3 Chart Workspace Object Model

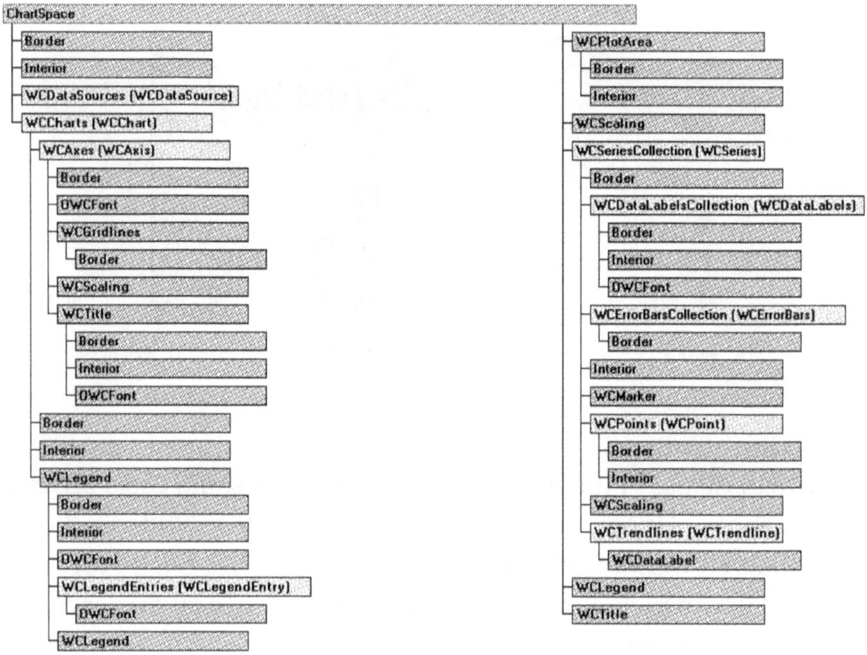

The Chart Area

The Chart Area is an object that contains all other elements in the chart. You can think of it as a chart's master background.

In OWC, ChartSpace object represents the chart workspace. The chart workspace is the top-level chart container; it can contain more than one chart, with each chart represented by a WCChart object. When a chart workspace is first created, it is empty (it does not contain any charts). Use the Add method of the WCChart object to create a new chart. Using the ChartSpace Object you can use either the CreateObject method or the New keyword to create a new ChartSpace object.

The object ID for a chart control on an HTML page or a Visual Basic form returns a ChartSpace object.

The programmatic identifier for the ChartSpace object is CLSID:0002E500-0000-0000-C000-000000000046.

The following example creates a chart workspace named "ChartSpace1" on an HTML page:

```
<object  id=ChartSpace1  classid=CLSID:0002E500-0000-0000-
C000-000000000046 style="width:100%;height:350"></object>
```

When you create a new ChartSpace object, it initially does not contain any charts. To add a chart to the ChartSpace object, use the Add method of the WCCharts collection.

Table 2.2: Property and Method for ChartSpace object

Property or Method	Description
ChartSpace.Charts	This property returns the WCCharts collection of all the WCChart objects in the Chart control.
WCCharts.Add	Use this method to add a new chart to the chart space.
ChartSpace.Clear	This method clears all content from the Chart control. Use it to quickly remove all charts, data sources, and any other elements within the chart space.

The Plot Area

The Chart Area of a chart contains the Plot Area, which is the part of the chart that contains the actual chart. In OWC, WCPlotArea Object represents the plot area on a chart (the area where the chart data is plotted). Pie, doughnut, radar, and polar charts *do not* have a plot area; instead, these charts draw directly on the chart area. The WCChart object's PlotArea property returns a WCPlotArea object. PlotArea Property returns a WCPlotArea object that represents the plot area on the specified chart.

Figure 2.4: Sample Chart Elements Illustration

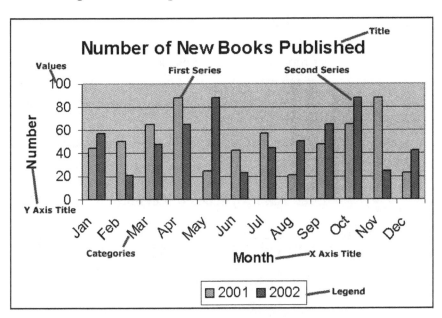

Chart Titles

A chart can have as many as five different titles (see Figure 2.4):
—Chart title
—Category X axis title
—Value Y axis title
—Second category X axis title
—Second category Y axis title

Some chart title properties:
> Font: change the font, size, color and attributes
> Position: adjust the vertical and horizontal alignment and orientation

Legend

A chart's legend consists of text and keys. A key is a small graphic that corresponds to the chart's series (see Figure 2.4).

WCLegend object represents a chart workspace or chart legend. A chart or chart workspace can have only one legend. The WCLegend object contains a WCLegendEntries collection that contains one or more WCLegendEntry objects.

You might want to hide or show the legend of a chart or hide individual legend entries. To do so, use the following properties:

Table 2.3: Properties of Legend

Property	Description
ChartSpace.HasChartSpaceLegend, WCChart.HasLegend	Like the WCAxis.HasTitle property described above, the HasChartSpaceLegend and HasLEgend properties determine whether the chart space and individual chart will show and reserve space for a legend. To use the ChartSpcaceLegend or Legend property described below, first set the HasChartSpaceLegend or Has Legend property to True.
ChartSpace.ChartSpaceLegend, WCChart.Legend	The ChartSpaceLegend and Legend peoperties return WCLegend objects that represent the legends for the entire chart space and the individual chart, respectively.
WCLegend.LegendEntries	This property returns the WCLegendEntries collection of all entries in the legend. The collection has a Count property that tells you how many entries appear in the legend and an Item property that lets you retrieve each one.
WCLegendEntry.Visible	This property determines whether a legend entry apprears in the legend. Setting this to False will hide the legend entry.
WCLegend.Position	This property determines where the legend is placed in the chart. It can be place on the top, bottom, left side, or right side (the default) of the chart.

Series

A series represents a sequence of data points that you want to display in a certain manner. Most of the OWC Chart component internal structures are oriented around the series. Each series correlates to an entry in the chart's legend.

In the chart above we have two series: 2001 and 2002. The 2001 series has different color than the 2002 series. The legend corresponds to our series.

The WCSeries object is a member of the WCSeriesCollection collection. To add a series into series collection of the chart object, we can use the following syntax:

```
oChart.Charts(0).SeriesCollection.Add
```

We can also set or returns the type for a single series in a chart by using Type property:

Table 2.4: Type Property of Series

Property	Description
WCSeries.Type	This property sets or returns the type for a single series in a chart. Multiple series can each have their own type, but not all types can be combined in one chart.

Values

When loading the chart with literal data, the data can be contained either in an array of variants or in a tab-delimited string, each element or token representing a different value.

The SetData method is used to pass the literal data, but note that the second argument (normally the data source index) is the constant chDataLiteral. This constant, which is equal to -1, tells the chart that the next argument is literal data and not part of a data source.

You must use the SetData method of the WCSeries object (the object representing a series) when passing literal values to the chart. Since the Chart control itself can accept only a one-dimensional array of values, if it allowed you to pass literal values to the SetData method of the WCChart object (the object representing a chart), it would have no way of knowing which values belong to which series. The previous procedure handles this by simply looping through the series collection and passing the appropriate array of values to the current series SetData method.

Table 2.5: SetData Method

Method	Description
WCChart.SetData	This method can be used to load data into the entire chart at once, including series names.
WCSeries.SetData	This method loads data into a given series.

Axes

Charts vary in the number of axis that they use. Pie and doughnut chart have no axes. Other charts have two axes (three, if you use a secondary-value axis; four, if you use a secondary-category axis in an XY Scatter chart).

Often you will want to adjust the look of the various axes in your chart.

Table 2.6: Properties of Axes

Property	Description
WCChart.Axes	This property returns the WCAxes collection, from which you can obtain a specific axis. To ask for an axis by its location, use the appropriate constant from ChartAxisPositionEnum. To retrieve the axes in order, use their index values.
WCAxis.NumberFormat	This property sets or returns the number format used for value axis labels. You can specify any number format that the Spreadsheet control supports, including the named formats and the custom formats.
WCAxis.Font	This property returns the OWCfont object for the axis. You can use the properties of this object to adjust the name, size, and other font attributes of the axis labels.
WCAxis.HasTitle	This property sets or returns whether the axis has a title. If this property is False, no title exists; the space it would have used is reclaimed for the chart. If this property is set to True, the axis will have a title; you can use the WCAxis.Title property to get at the WCTitle object and set its caption. Note that accessing the Title property while WCAxis.HasTitle is False results in a run-time error.
WCAxis.Title	This property returns the WCTitle object for the axis, with which you can set the title's caption, font, and color settings.
WCAxis.TickLabelSpacing	This property sets or returns the tick label spacing determines how many labels are dropped from the axis between those that are displayed. This technique is useful for dropping date values when you have too many to show. The dropped labels can be assumed base on the surrounding labels.
WCAxis.TickMarkSpacing	This property sets or returns the spacing between tick marks on an axis. Like the TickLabelSpacing property, this property determines how many tick marks should be dropped between those that are shown.

Gridlines

Gridlines can help you to determine what the chart series represents numerically. Gridlines simply extend the tick marks on the axes. Some charts look better with gridlines; others appear more cluttered. You cannot have gridlines without an axis. Gridlines extend the tick marks on a chart axis to make it easier to see the values associated with the data markers. This object is not a collection. There is no object that represents a single gridline; you either have all gridlines for an axis turned on or all of them turned off.

MajorGridlines Property represents the major gridlines for the specified axis; MinorGridlines Property represents the minor gridlines for the specified axis. Note that you can use gridlines on any axis.

Error Bars

For certain chart types, you can add error bars to your chart. Error bars often are used to indicate "plus or minus" information that reflects uncertainty in the data. Error bars are appropriate only for area, bar, column, line and XY charts.

There are several types of error bars:

➤ Fixed value: The error bars are fixed by an amount that you specify
➤ Percentage: the error bars are a percentage of each value
➤ Standard deviation: the error bars are in the number of standard-deviation units that you specify
➤ Standard error: the error bars are one standard error unit
➤ Custom: the error bar units for the upper or lower error bars are set by you.

Figure 2.5: Error Bars with Fixed Value

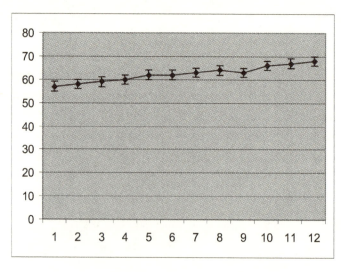

Trendline

A trendline points out general trends in your data. In some cases, you can forecast future data with trendlines. The following chart has no trendline:

Figure 2.6: A Series of Values without Trendline

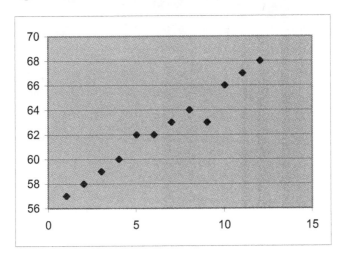

After we added linear trendline to the same chart, it will looks like this:

Figure 2.7: A Series of Values with Trendline

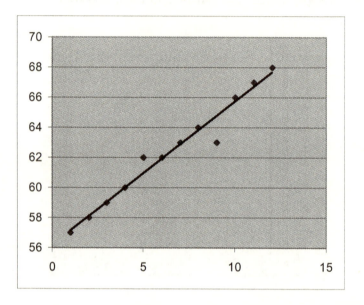

A trendline is used to show the trend of data in a series. Trendlines are commonly used in trend analysis and forecasting when you want to predict what a certain value will be in the future if it keep increasing or decreasing at the historical rate.

Data labels

A data label shows the value of each data point. You can also use data labels to show percentage in the series, category name, series name, or bubble size. You can also use data labels to display any combination of these. In addition, you can format the font, color, border attributes, and separator character to use between each piece of information in the data labels.

Data labels are very useful to present the numbers for comparison and analysis between different data points:

Figure 2.8: Data Labels for Column Chart

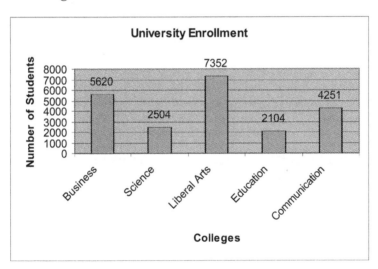

You can also use data labels to show the percentage of each category in pie chart:

Figure 2.9: Data Labels for Pie Chart

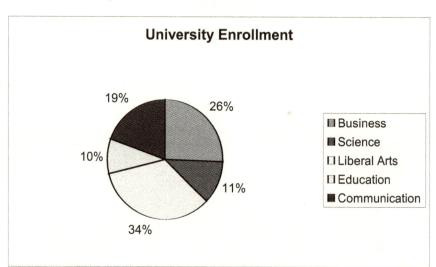

Data labels are attached to a series—just like trendlines and error bars,. You can not format, hide, or show a data label for an individual data point. All manipulations to data labels will affect all data points in the same series.

Summary

In this chapter we had a brief overview of all chart types that supported by OWC chart component and elements of chart. The following chapter will actually illustrate how to construct all different types of charts that even include combination chart.

Although the default settings for chart elements considers as good layout. Sometimes you may need to format the element to meet your specific need. Therefore, you need to overwrite the default setting by explicitly set the element properties or methods to the values you need.

Chapter 3

Programming Chart Component

In this chapter we will go through all chart types and show you the code of how to construct them. All data will load from the SQL Server database at run time and we use dynamic array to hold all values. We use DSN less OLE DB database connection. For more information on ASP databases, please check out other books on this topic and/or along with the brief introduction in chapter 1 if you do not familiar with this topic. Please change all server name, database name, login id, and password to your specific database settings. After we retrieved data from the database, we use the chart component to draw charts from the array values.

Due to its usefulness, I even included Gantt chart into this chapter even Gantt Chart is not a OWC chart type. But programmers often need to construct Gantt chart to display project schedule and provide task management chart. Therefore, this reference will be useful for programmers who need to construct Gantt chart in their applications.

Pie Chart

Introduction to Pie Chart

A pie chart shows the proportional size of items that make up of a data series to the sum of the items. It always shows only one data series and is useful when you want to emphasize a significant element.

Regular pie chart looks like an uncut pie. Exploded pie chart looks like a sliced pie and there is a space between each slice.

Here is a regular pie chart example:

Figure 3.1: Simple Pie Chart

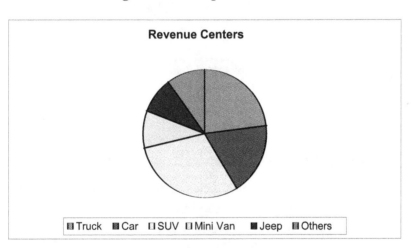

Here is a exploded pie chart example.

Figure 3.2: Exploded Pie Chart

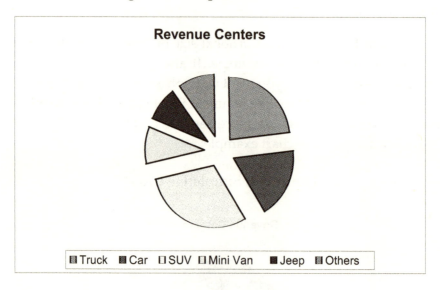

Pie Chart Properties

Pie chart can have two properties: categories and corresponding values for each category. For example, a car dealer has the following table to create a pie chart as above examples:

Table "RevenueCenter" has fields of Category and Data.

Table 3.1: "RevenueCenter"

Category	Data
Truck	46052
Car	36985
SUV	58213
Mini Van	20154
Jeep	18246
Others	19229

Therefore the car dealer has six categories: truck, car, SUV, mini van, jeep, and others. Each category has its corresponding values. The pie chart will show each category as a slice of the pie according to its proportion to the sum of all categories. Pie chart has its advantage of showing which category is significant to the overall result. In this case, we can see clearly that SUV is our leader out of all the revenue centers. Pie chart is simple and straightforward. But it is also lack of information. Because pie chart is a single series graph, the pie chart legend will show category titles. Most other charts will show series on their legends.

It is almost identical to construct a pie chart or exploded pie chart. The only difference is the Chart Type constant value needs to be changed in the chart declaration section. Here are the constants for both chart types:

Table 3.2: Pie Chart Constants

Chart Type	Constants
Pie Chart	ChartTypePie
Exploded Pie	ChartTypePieExploded

There are four options available for legend positions: left, right, top, bottom. You can use either string or integer value to control the legend position. Here is the table that shows the four options:

Table 3.3: Legend Positions

Position	Constant String	Constant Integer
Right	LegendPositionRight	0
Top	LegendPositionTop	1
Bottom	LegendPositionBottom	2
Left	LegendPositionLeft	3

For example, you can set the legend position to bottom by using:

```
<%
oChart.Charts(0).Legend.Position = c.chLegendPositionBottom
%>
```

Or you can use:

```
<%
oChart.Charts(0).Legend.Position = 2
%>
```

Both of the syntax are correct and give you the same results.

Please note legend position is not only apply to the pie chart, it applies to other chart types as well.

Construct Pie Chart

First, before we start any coding, use Option Explicit declaration. Option Explicit requires that we declare all variables before we use them. This is very important in ASP programming. It will helps to speed up the performance, avoid typos, and create robust code.

```
<% Option Explicit %>
```

Second, we need to create a OWC chart object. If we use the data from a database, we also need to create a database connection to retrieve the data from our database then assign those values into the chart object.

We declare oChart as OWC chart object, c as a shortcut for oChart constants. All categories will be stored in the Categories array and all corresponding values will be stored in the Vals array. In order to store all values into the array dynamically, we declare an array length counter lngCounter so this counter will increment with each record set loop. Our chart will need a caption, so we declare sCaption as our string holder for caption characters.

```
<%
Dim oChart, c, Categories(), Vals(), lngCounter, sCaption
%>
```

Then we establish database connection by declaring database connection variables and SQL string variable. We need to retrieve data from RevenueCenter table. After we get our record set, we can assign Categories into the category array and assign data into the Vals array.

```
<%
Dim oConn, objRS, strSQL, strConn

set oConn=Server.CreateObject("ADODB.connection")
set objRS=Server.CreateObject("ADODB.recordset")

strConn = "driver=SQL Server;server=YourServer;"
strConn = strConn & "database=YourDatabase;uid=YourUserID;
pwd=YourPassword;"

oConn.ConnectionString = strConn
oConn.Open

strSQL = "SELECT * FROM RevenueCenter"

'Open recordset using SQL string above
```

```
objRS.Open strSQL, oConn

'Clear all arrays and length counter variable

ReDim Categories(0)
ReDim Vals(0)
lngCounter = 0

'Loop through the record set to assign each category and values
into arrays
While Not objRS.EOF
    ReDim Preserve Categories(lngCounter)
    ReDim Preserve Vals(lngCounter)
    Categories(lngCounter) = CStr(objRS("Category"))
    If objRS("Data") <> "" Then
            Vals(lngCounter) = objRS("Data")
    Else
            Vals(lngCounter) = 0
    End If
    lngCounter = lngCounter + 1
    objRS.MoveNext
Wend

'Clean up the database connection

objRS.Close
Set objRS = Nothing
oConn.Close
Set oConn = Nothing
%>
```

You may have noticed that we have to ReDim and Preserve array values since we built two dynamic arrays for category and values. Each time before we move to the next record, we have to increase the array length counter by 1 so each array value has its unique identifier to avoid overwrite each other.

Since we have successfully stored our revenue table into our arrays. Now we are ready to create our pie chart. We set oChart as OWC chart object and set c as oChart constants shortcut. The c shortcut is very handy for simplify our code. This will make our job much easier to specify our chart properties later. Then we set our border to none. You can set to other color, but I feel it is more comfortable with no border color. Then we add a chart to the chart object and declare its chart type as regular pie chart. If you want to change it to explode pie chart, you just have to change it to chChartTypePieExplode.

```
<%
Set oChart = Server.CreateObject("OWC.Chart")
Set c = oChart.Constants

oChart.Border.Color = c.chColorNone

sCaption = "Revenue Centers"

oChart.Charts.Add
oChart.Charts(0).Type = oChart.Constants.chChartTypePie
%>
```

We add our arrays into the chart series collection. Then we add chart title from sCaption string. The variable fnt is a shortcut of font property. We declare sFname as our file name holder. Finally, we put our legend to the bottom and declare our graphic size as 400 pixels wide and 400 pixels in height. Once we exported our graphic, we can display it on our web page.

```
<%
oChart.Charts(0).SeriesCollection.Add
oChart.Charts(0).SeriesCollection(0).Border.Color = "black"
oChart.Charts(0).SeriesCollection(0).SetData
c.chDimCategories, c.chDataLiteral, Categories
oChart.Charts(0).SeriesCollection(0).SetData c.chDimValues,
c.chDataLiteral, Vals
```

```
oChart.Charts(0).HasTitle = True
oChart.Charts(0).SeriesCollection(0).Caption = sCaption

Dim fnt, sFname

set fnt = oChart.Charts(0).Title.Font
fnt.Name = "arial"
fnt.Size = 14
fnt.Bold = True

oChart.Charts(0).PlotArea.Interior.Color = "#CCCC99"
oChart.Charts(0).HasLegend = True
oChart.Charts(0).Legend.Position = c.chLegendPositionBottom
oChart.Charts(0).Legend.Font = "Tahoma"
oChart.Charts(0).Legend.Font.size = 7
oChart.Charts(0).Legend.LegendEntries(0).Visible = True

sFname = "Tempchart.gif"

oChart.ExportPicture server.MapPath(sFname), "gif", 400, 400

Response.Write "<tr><td><img align='top' src='" & sFname &
"'></td></tr></table>"
%>
```

Here is our complete code with comments in it:

```
<%@ language="vbscript" %>
<% Option Explicit %>
<html>
<head>
   <title>Pie Chart Example</title>
</head>
<body>
<Table align="left" width="100%">
<%
Dim oChart, c, Categories(), Vals(), lngCounter, sCaption

Dim oConn, objRS, strSQL, strConn
```

```
set oConn=Server.CreateObject("ADODB.connection")
set objRS=Server.CreateObject("ADODB.recordset")

strConn = "driver=SQL Server;server=YourServer;"
strConn = strConn & "database=YourDatabase;uid=YourUserID;
pwd=YourPassword;"

oConn.ConnectionString = strConn
oConn.Open

strSQL = "SELECT * FROM RevenueCenter"

'Open recordset using SQL string above

objRS.Open strSQL, oConn

'Clear all arrays and length counter variable

ReDim Categories(0)
ReDim Vals(0)
lngCounter = 0

'Loop through the record set to assign each category and
values into arrays

While Not objRS.EOF
   ReDim Preserve Categories(lngCounter)
   ReDim Preserve Vals(lngCounter)
   Categories(lngCounter) = CStr(objRS("Category"))
   If objRS("Data") <> "" Then
         Vals(lngCounter) = objRS("Data")
   Else
         Vals(lngCounter) = 0
   End If
   lngCounter = lngCounter + 1
   objRS.MoveNext
Wend

'Clean up the database connection
```

```
objRS.Close
Set objRS = Nothing
oConn.Close
Set oConn = Nothing

' Create a Chart Object
Set oChart = Server.CreateObject("OWC.Chart")
Set c = oChart.Constants

oChart.Border.Color = c.chColorNone

sCaption = "Revenue Centers"

oChart.Charts.Add
oChart.Charts(0).Type = oChart.Constants.chChartTypePie
oChart.Charts(0).SeriesCollection.Add

oChart.Charts(0).SeriesCollection(0).Border.Color = "black"

oChart.Charts(0).SeriesCollection(0).SetData
c.chDimCategories, c.chDataLiteral, Categories
oChart.Charts(0).SeriesCollection(0).SetData c.chDimValues,
c.chDataLiteral, Vals

' Declare chart title and take sCaption as title string
oChart.Charts(0).HasTitle = True
oChart.Charts(0).SeriesCollection(0).Caption = sCaption

Dim fnt, sFname

' Set title font size and other properties

set fnt = oChart.Charts(0).Title.Font
fnt.Name = "arial"
fnt.Size = 14
fnt.Bold = True

oChart.Charts(0).PlotArea.Interior.Color = "#CCCC99"
oChart.Charts(0).HasLegend = True
oChart.Charts(0).Legend.Position = c.chLegendPositionBottom
```

```
oChart.Charts(0).Legend.Font = "Tahoma"
oChart.Charts(0).Legend.Font.size = 7
oChart.Charts(0).Legend.LegendEntries(0).Visible = True

sFname = "Tempchart.gif"

oChart.ExportPicture server.MapPath(sFname), "gif", 400, 400

' Create a link to the generated file
Response.Write "<tr><td><img align='top' src='" & sFname &
"'></td></tr></table>"
%>
</body>
</html>
```

When we run our code (assume our database table has been properly set up), we should get the following chart displays on the web page:

Figure 3.3: Pie Chart

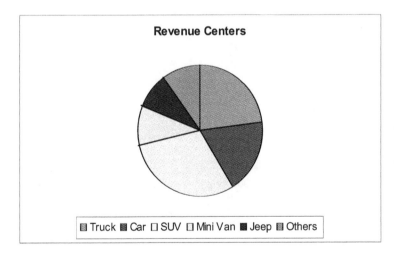

Line Chart

Regular Line Chart

A line chart shows trends in data at equal intervals. Line chart is more useful when its categories are in meaningful order such as dates or time. If you use a line chart to show sales volume in 2001, with a sequential time interval of monthly or quarterly will allow user to see the volume change throughout the year:

Figure 3.4: Regular Line Chart

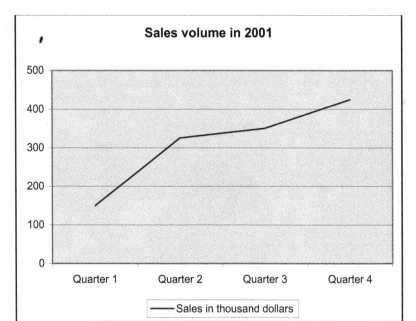

The process of creating a regular line chart is very similar to create a pie chart. To create the line chart as above, we first need to get the data from database table. Table "Sales" has the following records:

Table 3.4: Sales Table

Category	Data
Quarter 1	150
Quarter 2	325
Quarter 3	350
Quarter 4	425

Therefore, we need to create two arrays, one for category and another one for sales data:

```
<%
Dim Categories(), Vals()
%>
```

After we established the database connection, we can assign Categories into the category array and assign data into the Vals array. We use ReDim and Preserve to hold the previous array values.

```
<%
While Not objRS.EOF
    ReDim Preserve Categories(lngCounter)
    ReDim Preserve Vals(lngCounter)
    Categories(lngCounter) = CStr(objRS("Category"))
    If objRS("Data") <> "" Then
        Vals(lngCounter) = objRS("Data")
    Else
        Vals(lngCounter) = 0
    End If
    lngCounter = lngCounter + 1
    objRS.MoveNext
Wend
%>
```

To create a line chart, we declare the chart type as line chart:

```
<%
oChart.Charts.Add
oChart.Charts(0).Type = oChart.Constants.chChartTypeLine
%>
```

Here is the complete code section for line chart that shown above:

```
<%
Dim oChart, c
Dim Categories(), Vals()
Dim lngCounter, fnt, sFname
Dim oConn, objRS, strSQL, strConn

set oConn=Server.CreateObject("ADODB.connection")
set objRS=Server.CreateObject("ADODB.recordset")

strConn = "driver=SQL Server;server=YourServer;"
strConn = strConn & "database=YourDatabase;uid=YourUserID;
pwd=YourPassword;"

oConn.ConnectionString = strConn
oConn.Open

strSQL = "SELECT * FROM RevenueCenter"

'Open recordset using SQL string above

objRS.Open strSQL, oConn

'Clear all arrays and length counter variable

ReDim Categories(0)
ReDim Vals(0)
lngCounter = 0

'Loop through the record set to assign each category and
values into arrays
```

```
While Not objRS.EOF
   ReDim Preserve Categories(lngCounter)
   ReDim Preserve Vals(lngCounter)
   Categories(lngCounter) = CStr(objRS("Category"))
   If objRS("Data") <> "" Then
         Vals(lngCounter) = objRS("Data")
   Else
         Vals(lngCounter) = 0
   End If
   lngCounter = lngCounter + 1
   objRS.MoveNext
Wend

'Clean up the database connection

objRS.Close
Set objRS = Nothing
oConn.Close
Set oConn = Nothing

' Create a Chart Object
Set oChart = Server.CreateObject("OWC.Chart")
Set c = oChart.Constants

oChart.Border.Color = c.chColorNone

oChart.Charts.Add
oChart.Charts(0).Type = oChart.Constants.chChartTypeLine
oChart.Charts(0).SeriesCollection.Add

oChart.Charts(0).SeriesCollection(0).Border.Color = "black"
oChart.Charts(0).SeriesCollection(0).SetData
c.chDimCategories, c.chDataLiteral, Categories
oChart.Charts(0).SeriesCollection(0).SetData c.chDimValues,
c.chDataLiteral, Vals
oChart.Charts(0).SeriesCollection(0).Caption  =  "Sales  in
thousand dollars"
```

```
oChart.Charts(0).HasTitle = True
oChart.Charts(0).Title.Caption = "Sales Volume in 2001"
   set fnt = oChart.Charts(0).Title.Font
   fnt.Name = "arial"
   fnt.Size = 14
   fnt.Bold = True

oChart.Charts(0).PlotArea.Interior.Color = "#CCCC99"
oChart.Charts(0).HasLegend = True
oChart.Charts(0).Legend.Position = c.chLegendPositionBottom
oChart.Charts(0).Legend.Font = "Tahoma"
oChart.Charts(0).Legend.Font.size = 7

oChart.Charts(0).Legend.LegendEntries(0).Visible = True

'sFname = Session("FSO").GetTempName & session.SessionID &
".gif"
sFname = "Tempchart.gif"

oChart.ExportPicture  server.MapPath(sFname),  "gif",  400,
400

' Create a link to the generated file
Response.Write "<tr><td><img align='top' src='" & sFname &
"'></td></tr></table>"
%>
```

Line Chart with Markers

In order to highlight the significant points on the line chart, we can create a line chart with markers (Figure 3.5). Each markers has the value of the significant points so they looks more obvious on the line chart.

Figure 3.5: Line Chart with Markers

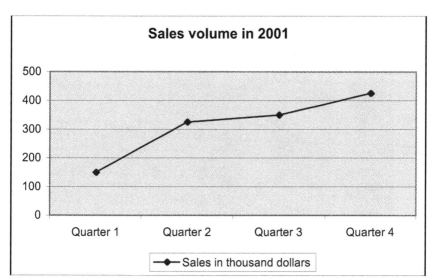

To create the chart as above, we can simply change the chart type from the above code to:

```
<%
oChart.Charts(0).Type = oChart.Constants.chChartTypeLineMarkers
%>
```

Stacked Line chart

Stacked line chart contains more than one lines. Each line is an individual series. Therefore, stacked line chart has multiple series.

Figure 3.6: Stacked Line Chart

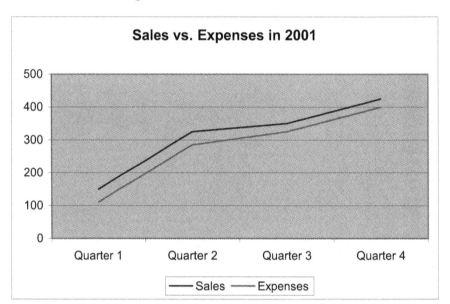

To create a stacked line chart above, we need to add another series that represent the expenses into the database. You may think our table should looks like this:

Table 3.5: Sale_Expense Table

	Sales	Expenses
Quarter 1	150	111
Quarter 2	325	285
Quarter 3	350	325
Quarter 4	425	400

This is an important point you have to remember when trying to draw stacked line chart: the first series is the baseline; the second series is the difference from the baseline.

In this case, we have to create a second series for expenses. First we have to declare an array to hold the second series values:

```
<%
Dim Expenses()
%>
```

Then we ReDim it and preserve it when loop through the record set just like the array for sales:

```
<%
ReDim Expenses(0)

Do While Not objRS.EOF
    ReDim Preserve Expenses(lngCounter)

    If objRS("Expenses") <> "" Then
            Expenses(lngCounter) = objRS("Expenses")
    Else
            Expenses(lngCounter) = 0
    End If

    lngCounter = lngCounter + 1
    objRS.MoveNext
Loop
%>
```

In order to display the expenses, we have to add another series into the chart object:

```
<%
oChart.Charts(0).SeriesCollection.Add
oChart.Charts(0).SeriesCollection(1).SetData c.chDimValues,
c.chDataLiteral, Expenses
%>
```

The sales series is SeriesCollection(0), so the expenses is SeriesCollection(1). You have to put oChart.Charts(0).SeriesCollection. Add before you can assign expenses values to the second series. Otherwise you will get an error message. You have to add this statement for every series you want to add.

Here is the complete code sample for two series sales vs. expenses line chart:

```
<%@ language="vbscript" %>
<% Option Explicit %>

<html>
<body>
<%
Dim oChart, c, Categories(), Vals(), Expenses(), lngCounter,
fnt, sFname
Dim oConn, objRS, strSQL, strConn

set oConn=Server.CreateObject("ADODB.connection")
set objRS=Server.CreateObject("ADODB.recordset")

strConn = "driver=SQL Server;server=YourServer;"
strConn = strConn & "database=YourDatabase;uid=YourUserID;
pwd=YourPassword;"

oConn.ConnectionString = strConn
oConn.Open

strSQL = "SELECT * FROM Sale_Expense"

'Open recordset using SQL string above

objRS.Open strSQL, oConn

'Clear all arrays and length counter variable
```

```
ReDim Categories(0)
ReDim Vals(0)
ReDim Expenses(0)
lngCounter = 0

'Loop through the record set to assign each category and
values into arrays

While Not objRS.EOF
   ReDim Preserve Categories(lngCounter)
   ReDim Preserve Vals(lngCounter)
   ReDim Preserve Expenses(lngCounter)
   Categories(lngCounter) = CStr(objRS("Category"))
   If objRS("Data") <> "" Then
        Vals(lngCounter) = objRS("Data")
   Else
        Vals(lngCounter) = 0
   End If
   If objRS("Expenses") <> "" Then
        Expenses(lngCounter) = objRS("Expenses")
   Else
        Expenses(lngCounter) = 0
   End If

   lngCounter = lngCounter + 1
   objRS.MoveNext
Wend

'Clean up the database connection

objRS.Close
Set objRS = Nothing
oConn.Close
Set oConn = Nothing
```

```
' Create a Chart Object
Set oChart = Server.CreateObject("OWC.Chart")
Set c = oChart.Constants

oChart.Border.Color = c.chColorNone

oChart.Charts.Add
oChart.Charts(0).Type = oChart.Constants.chChartTypeSmoothLine
oChart.Charts(0).SeriesCollection.Add
oChart.Charts(0).SeriesCollection(0).Border.Color = "black"
'Add series values
oChart.Charts(0).SeriesCollection(0).SetData
c.chDimCategories, c.chDataLiteral, Categories
oChart.Charts(0).SeriesCollection(0).SetData c.chDimValues,
c.chDataLiteral, Vals
oChart.Charts(0).SeriesCollection.Add
oChart.Charts(0).SeriesCollection(1).SetData c.chDimValues,
c.chDataLiteral, Expenses
'Add series titles
oChart.Charts(0).SeriesCollection(0).Caption = "Sales"
oChart.Charts(0).SeriesCollection(1).Caption = "Expenses"
'Format title
oChart.Charts(0).HasTitle = True
oChart.Charts(0).Title.Caption = "Sales vs. Expenses"
   set fnt = oChart.Charts(0).Title.Font
   fnt.Name = "arial"
   fnt.Size = 14
   fnt.Bold = True
'Format legend font and position
oChart.Charts(0).PlotArea.Interior.Color = "#CCCC99"
oChart.Charts(0).HasLegend = True
oChart.Charts(0).Legend.Position = c.chLegendPositionBottom
oChart.Charts(0).Legend.Font = "Tahoma"
oChart.Charts(0).Legend.Font.size = 7
oChart.Charts(0).Legend.LegendEntries(0).Visible = True
```

```
'Create a graph and specify the graph size
sFname = "Tempchart.gif"
oChart.ExportPicture server.MapPath(sFname), "gif", 400, 400

' Create a link to the generated file
Response.Write "<tr><td><img align='top' src='" & sFname &
"'></td></tr></table>"
%>
</body>
</html>
```

Stacked Line Chart with Markers and Two Other Line Charts

To create the same line chart with markers, just change this line of code from:

```
<%
oChart.Charts(0).Type = oChart.Constants.chChartTypeLineStacked
%>
```

To:

```
<%
oChart.Charts(0).Type =
oChart.Constants.chChartTypeLineStackedMarkers
%>
```

This will create a chart like this:

Figure 3.7: Stacked Line Chart with Markers

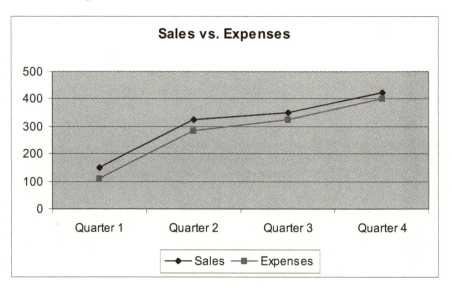

Another two types of line charts are: **100% stacked line chart** and **100% stacked markers line chart**. The 100% line charts display the trend of the percentage of each value contributes over time or categories. The Y axis shows the percentage instead of values. Here is the chart constants for those two charts, just modify the constants you are ready to go.

For 100% stacked line chart:

```
<%
oChart.Charts(0).Type = oChart.Constants.chChartTypeLineStacked100
%>
```

For 100% stacked markers line chart:

```
<%
oChart.Charts(0).Type =
oChart.Constants.chChartTypeLineStacked100Markers
%>
```

Smooth line chart

A smooth line chart shows trends in data at equal intervals, smoothed to show the estimated data between intervals. To create a smooth line chart use the following chart type declaration:

```
<%
oChart.Charts(0).Type = oChart.Constants.chChartTypeSmoothLine
%>
```

This will create a smooth line chart as below:

Figure 3.8 Smooth Line Chart

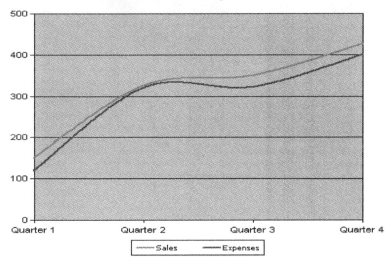

Area Chart

An area chart emphasizes the magnitude of change over time. By displaying the sum of the plotted values, an area chart also shows the relationship of parts to a whole. To create a area chart use the following chart type declaration:

```
<%
oChart.Charts(0).Type = oChart.Constants.chChartTypeArea
%>
```

This will create an area chart as below:

Figure 3.9 Regular Area Chart

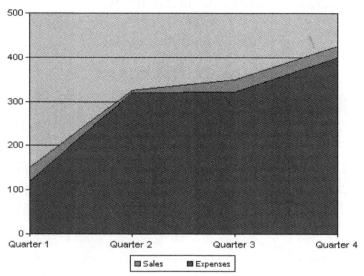

Stacked Area chart

An stacked area chart is useful to depict a visual total for each category. To create a stacked area chart use the following chart type declaration:

```
<%
oChart.Charts(0).Type = oChart.Constants.chChartTypeAreaStacked
%>
```

This will create a stacked area chart as below:

Figure 3.10 Stacked Area Chart

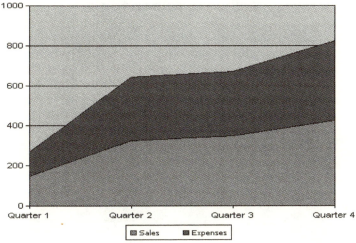

Sales vs. Expenses

100% Stacked Area chart

A 100% stacked area chart draws all the way across the plot area and then subdivides the area into segments representing the percent contribution of each series' data point. To create a 100% stacked area chart use the following chart type declaration:

```
<%
oChart.Charts(0).Type = oChart.Constants.chChartTypeAreaStacked100
%>
```

This will create a stacked area chart as below:

Figure 3.11 100% Stacked Area Chart

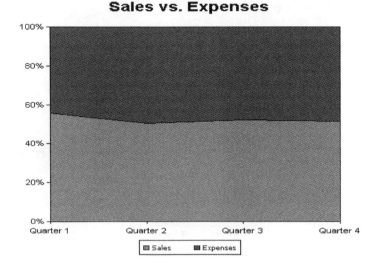

Column Chart & Bar Chart

Clustered Column Chart

The clustered column chart compares data across the categories. Column chart shows a filled bar for each data point, extending from the zero point on the value axis to the data point. Unlike line charts, column chart does not portray a sense of progression.

The following table shows the number of staffs in a hospital. Although the number of doctors has generally increased from 1998 to 2000, the number of nurses has been decreased over the same period of time due to national nurse shortage:

Table 3.6 Hospital Staff Table

Category	Doctors	Nurses
1998	155	377
1999	172	358
2000	180	350
2001	175	322

To create a column chart from this table, we need to create three arrays: one for years, one for the number of doctors, and one for the number of nurses:

```
<%
Dim Categories(), Doctors(), Nurses(), lngCounter
ReDim Categories(0)
ReDim Doctors(0)
ReDim Nurses(0)
lngCounter = 0
%>
```

While we loop through the record set, we assign the table values to these arrays accordingly and use ReDim and Preserve to hold the values in each array:

```
<%
Do While Not objRS.EOF
    ReDim Preserve Categories(lngCounter)
    ReDim Preserve Doctors(lngCounter)
    ReDim Preserve Nurses(lngCounter)
    Categories(lngCounter) = CStr(objRS("Category"))
    If objRS("Doctors") <> "" Then
            Doctors(lngCounter) = objRS("Doctors")
    Else
            Doctors(lngCounter) = 0
    End If
    If objRS("Nurses") <> "" Then
            Nurses(lngCounter) = objRS("Nurses")
    Else
            Nurses(lngCounter) = 0
    End If
    lngCounter = lngCounter + 1
    objRS.MoveNext
Loop
%>
```

Just like other chart types we have described earlier, we have to specify the chart type as clustered column chart:

```
<%
oChart.Charts.Add
Chart.Charts(0).Type = oChart.Constants.chChartTypeColumnClustered
%>
```

Since clustered column chart has two series in this case (doctors and nurses), we have to add both of them to the chart object:

```
<%
oChart.Charts(0).SeriesCollection(0).SetData
c.chDimCategories, c.chDataLiteral, Categories
oChart.Charts(0).SeriesCollection(0).SetData c.chDimValues,
c.chDataLiteral, Doctors
oChart.Charts(0).SeriesCollection.Add
oChart.Charts(0).SeriesCollection(1).SetData c.chDimValues,
c.chDataLiteral, Nurses
%>
```

The whole code section looks like this:

```
<%@ language="vbscript" %>
<% Option Explicit %>
<html>
<body>
<Table align="left" width="100%">
<%

Dim oChart, c, Categories(), Doctors(), Nurses(), lngCounter,
fnt, sFname
Dim oABCData1, oABCConn1, sSQL1, rsResults1

Set oABCData1 = CreateObject("ABCDataLayer.DBAccess")
Set oABCConn1 = oABCData1.OpenABCConnection(DB_CONNECTION_STRING)

sSQL1 = "SELECT * FROM Staff"

Set rsResults1 = oABCData1.ExecuteSQL(sSQL1, oABCConn1)

ReDim Categories(0)
ReDim Doctors(0)
ReDim Nurses(0)
lngCounter = 0
```

```
'Loop through the record set

Do While Not rsResults1.EOF
   ReDim Preserve Categories(lngCounter)
   ReDim Preserve Doctors(lngCounter)
   ReDim Preserve Nurses(lngCounter)
   Categories(lngCounter) = CStr(rsResults1("Category"))
   If rsResults1("Doctors") <> "" Then
        Doctors(lngCounter) = rsResults1("Doctors")
   Else
        Doctors(lngCounter) = 0
   End If
   If rsResults1("Nurses") <> "" Then
        Nurses(lngCounter) = rsResults1("Nurses")
   Else
        Nurses(lngCounter) = 0
   End If
   lngCounter = lngCounter + 1
   rsResults1.MoveNext
Loop

'Cleanup the record set
rsResults1.Close
Set rsResults1 = Nothing
oABCData1.CloseABCConnection oABCConn1
Set oABCData1 = Nothing

' Create a Chart Object
Set oChart = Server.CreateObject("OWC.Chart")
Set c = oChart.Constants

oChart.Border.Color = c.chColorNone

oChart.Charts.Add
oChart.Charts(0).Type = oChart.Constants.chChartTypeColumnClustered
oChart.Charts(0).SeriesCollection.Add
oChart.Charts(0).SeriesCollection(0).Border.Color = "black"
```

```
'Add series values
oChart.Charts(0).SeriesCollection(0).SetData
c.chDimCategories, c.chDataLiteral, Categories
oChart.Charts(0).SeriesCollection(0).SetData c.chDimValues,
c.chDataLiteral, Doctors
oChart.Charts(0).SeriesCollection.Add
oChart.Charts(0).SeriesCollection(1).SetData c.chDimValues,
c.chDataLiteral, Nurses
'Add series titles
oChart.Charts(0).SeriesCollection(0).Caption = "Doctors"
oChart.Charts(0).SeriesCollection(1).Caption = "Nurses"
'Format title
oChart.Charts(0).HasTitle = True
oChart.Charts(0).Title.Caption = "Number of Doctors and Nurses"
   set fnt = oChart.Charts(0).Title.Font
   fnt.Name = "arial"
   fnt.Size = 14
   fnt.Bold = True
'Format legend font and position
oChart.Charts(0).PlotArea.Interior.Color = "#CCCC99"
oChart.Charts(0).HasLegend = True
oChart.Charts(0).Legend.Position = c.chLegendPositionBottom
oChart.Charts(0).Legend.Font = "Tahoma"
oChart.Charts(0).Legend.Font.size = 7
oChart.Charts(0).Legend.LegendEntries(0).Visible = True

'Create a graph and specify the graph size
sFname = "Tempchart.gif"
oChart.ExportPicture server.MapPath(sFname), "gif", 400, 400

' Create a link to the generated file
Response.Write "<tr><td><img align='top' src='" & sFname
Response.Write "'></td></tr></table>"
%>

</body>
</html>
```

The above code will produce the following chart on the web page:

Figure 3.12: Clustered Column Chart

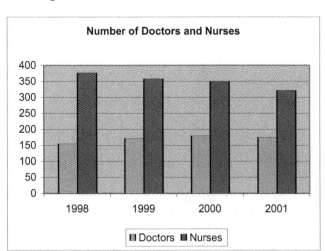

Stacked Column Chart

Stacked column chart display different series as stacked upon each other. In stacked column charts, the length of the column represents the sum of the data points for the category. The stacked column charts provide a useful overview for the total amount of each category. However, the stacked column charts does not depict the relative contribution of individual series as clear as regular column charts.

To create a stacked column chart from the data above, we only need to change the chart type:

```
<%
oChart.Charts.Add
Chart.Charts(0).Type = oChart.Constants.chChartTypeColumnStacked
%>
```

From the above code sample with this chart type modification, we can produce the following stacked column chart:

Figure 3.13: Stacked Column Chart

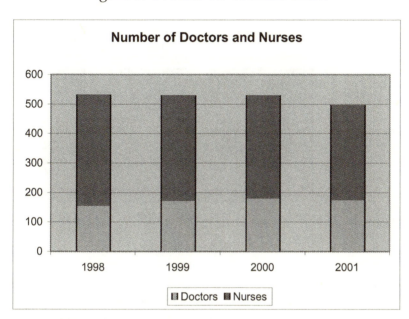

100% Stacked Column Chart

The 100% Stacked column chart compares the percentage each value contributes to a total across categories.

To create a stacked column chart from the data above, we only need to change the chart type:

```
<%
oChart.Charts.Add
Chart.Charts(0).Type = oChart.Constants.chChartTypeColumnStacked100
%>
```

From the above code sample with this chart type modification, we can produce the following stacked column chart:

Figure 3.14: 100% Stacked Column Chart

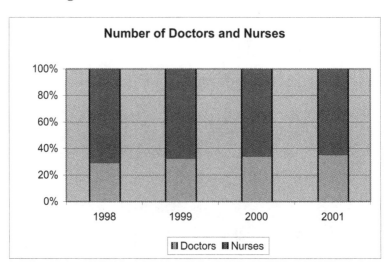

During this time frame, 100% stacked column chart has depicted the percentage of total number of doctors for the hospital staff is increasing.

Bar Chart

A bar chart illustrates comparisons among individual items. To focus on comparing values and to place less emphasis on time, categories are organized vertically and values are organized horizontally.

The reason we group bar chart and column chart into one section is because they are very similar to each other, except they extend to different direction:

To create a bar chart from the data above, we only need to change the chart type:

```
<%
oChart.Charts.Add
Chart.Charts(0).Type = oChart.Constants.chChartTypeBarClustered
%>
```

From the above code sample with this chart type modification, we can produce the following bar chart:

Figure 3.15: Clustered Bar Chart

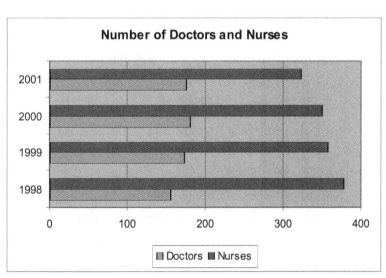

Stacked Bar Chart

Similar to stacked column chart, stacked bar chart shows the relationship of individual items to the whole.

To create a stacked bar chart from the data above, we only need to change the chart type:

```
<%
oChart.Charts.Add
Chart.Charts(0).Type = oChart.Constants.chChartTypeBarStacked
%>
```

From the above code sample with this chart type modification, we can produce the following stacked bar chart:

Figure 3.15: Stacked Bar Chart

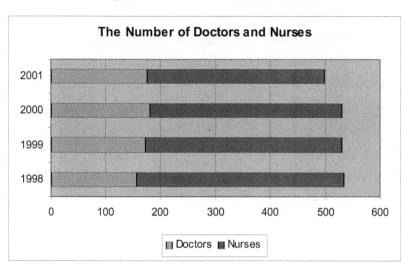

100% Stacked Bar Chart

The 100% stacked bar chart is also similar to 100% column chart compares the percentage each value contributes to a total across categories.

To create a stacked bar chart from the data above, we only need to change the chart type:

```
<%
oChart.Charts.Add
oChart.Charts(0).Type = oChart.Constants.chChartTypeBarStacked100
%>
```

From the above code sample with this chart type modification, we can produce the following stacked bar chart:

Figure 3.16: Stacked Bar Chart

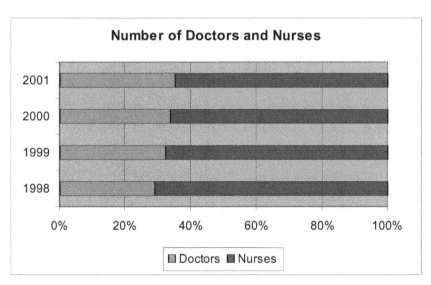

Gantt Chart

Introduction to Gantt Chart

Gantt chart is one of the most useful charts for project management purposes. Although there is not a chart type for Gantt chart in OWC Chart Component, we can borrow bar chart to create a Gantt chart. There are several elements are necessary for Gantt chart: task description for all the tasks involved the project on Y axis and dates on X axis to show the time frame for the project.

Our table has sequence number for each task, task description, starting date, and completion date. We need to draw a Gantt chart from this table.

Table 3. 7: Gantt Chart Table

SequenceNum	TaskDescription	DateOfStart	DateOf Completion
1	Leader Selection	08/14/00	09/01/00
2	Project Planning	09/02/00	09/14/00
3	Data Collection Launch	09/15/00	09/25/00
4	Lead Intensive	09/15/00	10/19/00
5	Senior Exec Briefing	10/20/00	12/05/00
6	TF Education (Launch)	12/05/00	02/10/01
7	Nurse Mgr Ed (Mgr Briefing)	02/12/01	02/24/01
8	RN/Mgr Focus Groups	02/25/01	03/07/01
9	RN/Mgr Preference Satisfaction Research	03/07/01	04/07/01
10	Data Analysis	04/07/01	05/01/01
11	Process Mapping Workshop/Tactic Selection	05/02/01	05/19/01

Here is the Gantt chart for a "Nurse Retention Project." From the Gantt chart, you can see this project starts after August, 2000 and it ends before June 8th, 2001. Some of the tasks takes longer than others. The TF Education (launch) is the most time consuming task during the project.

Figure 3.17: Stacked Bar Chart

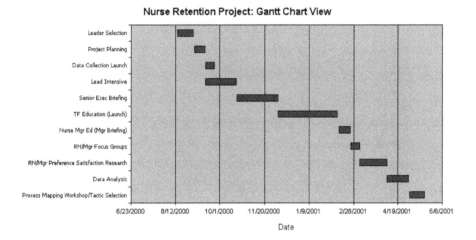

To create a Gantt chart, we need at three arrays: one for starting date of each task, one for date difference between starting date and ending date for each task, one for the name of each task:

```
<%
Dim arrStartDate(), arrDateDiff(), TaskName()
%>
```

While loop through the record set, we can ReDim and Preserve the values of each array. Since we are going to need starting date and ending date for the calculation, validate the existence of both dates are necessary to ensure we have no bad input:

```
<%
Do While Not rsResults.EOF
    ReDim Preserve arrStartDate(lngCounter)
    ReDim Preserve arrDateDiff(lngCounter)
    ReDim Preserve TaskName(lngCounter)

If ((rsResults("DateOfStart") <> "") And
(rsResults("DateOfCompletion") <> ""))
Then
    'Task starting date
    arrStartDate(lngCounter) = CDate(rsResults("DateOfStart"))
    'Task end date
    varEndDate = CDate(rsResults("DateOfCompletion"))
    'Date difference between ending date and starting date
    arrDateDiff(lngCounter) = DateDiff("d", arrStartDate(lngCounter),
    varEndDate))
    'Task label
    TaskName(lngCounter) = CStr(rsResults("TaskDescription"))
    lngCounter = lngCounter + 1

End If

    rsResults.MoveNext
Loop
%>
```

The DateDiff function is used to calculate the date difference between two dates, the first string "d" means day. Therefore, we are returns number of days difference between those two dates.

Here comes the tricky part. In order to display the Gantt chart using the chart type bar stacked, we must hide the first bar that draws from the beginning to the start date. We only need to show the second bar that draws from the starting date to the ending date. Therefore, we need to set the first series background and border color to none:

```
<%
oChart.Charts(0).SeriesCollection(0).Border.Color = c.chColorNone
oChart.Charts(0).SeriesCollection(0).Interior.Color = c.chColorNone
oChart.Charts(0).SeriesCollection(0).SetData c.chDimValues,
c.chDataLiteral, arrStartDate
%>
```

We also need to format the x axis data into date format:

```
<%
set ax = cht.Axes(c.chAxisPositionBottom)
ax.HasTitle = True
ax.Title.Caption = "Date"
ax.Title.Font.Name = "arial"
ax.Title.Font.Size = 10
ax.NumberFormat = "Short date"
%>
```

Of course, you can add more series and add legend into the Gantt chart to create a more complicated Gantt chart. Here is the complete code sample for creating the Gantt chart as above:

```
<%@ Language=VBScript %>
<% Option Explicit %>
<html>
<body>
<%
'Declare variables and arrays for the Gantt Chart
Dim arrStartDate(), arrDateDiff(), TaskName(), varEndDate,
lngCounter
```

```
Dim cht, ax, ay, fnt, sFname, sFullFileName
Dim oChart, c, varEngagementID

Set Session("chartdetail") = CreateObject("Scripting.Dictionary")

Dim oConn, rsResults, strSQL, strConn
set oConn=Server.CreateObject("ADODB.connection")
set rsResults=Server.CreateObject("ADODB.recordset")
strConn = "driver=SQL Server;server=YourServer;"
strConn = strConn & "database=YourDatabase;uid=YourUserID;
pwd=YourPassword;"

oConn.ConnectionString = strConn
oConn.Open

strSQL = "SELECT * FROM Gantt ORDER BY SequenceNum DESC"

'Open recordset using SQL string above

rsResults.Open strSQL, oConn

ReDim arrStartDate(0)
ReDim arrDateDiff(0)
ReDim TaskName(0)
lngCounter = 0

'Loop through the record set to get the values for all arrays

Do While Not rsResults.EOF
    ReDim Preserve arrStartDate(lngCounter)
    ReDim Preserve arrDateDiff(lngCounter)
    ReDim Preserve TaskName(lngCounter)

If ((rsResults("DateOfStart") <> "") And
(rsResults("DateOfCompletion") <> ""))
Then
    'Task starting date
    arrStartDate(lngCounter) = CDate(rsResults("DateOfStart"))
    'Task end date
```

```
        varEndDate = CDate(rsResults("DateOfCompletion"))
        'Date difference between ending date and starting date
        arrDateDiff(lngCounter) = abs(DateDiff("d",
        arrStartDate(lngCounter), varEndDate))
        'Task label
        TaskName(lngCounter) = CStr(rsResults("TaskDescription"))
        lngCounter = lngCounter + 1

End If
    rsResults.MoveNext
Loop

'— Cleanup
rsResults.Close
Set rsResults = Nothing
oConn.Close
Set oConn = Nothing

'Assign arrays into session variables
Session("chartdetail").add "DS.Categories", TaskName
Session("chartdetail").add "DS.SeriesName", TaskName

    '_____

'*** CREATE OWC CHART SECTION ****
    '_____

    ' Create a Chart Object
    Set oChart = Server.CreateObject("OWC.Chart")
    Set c = oChart.Constants
    oChart.Clear
    '_____

'*** DEFINE MISC CHART ITEMS ****
    '_____

    ' Set the different parameters for the ChartSpace
    oChart.Border.Color = c.chColorNone

    ' Add a chart and set parameters for the chart
    Set cht = oChart.Charts.Add
```

```
cht.Type = oChart.Constants.chChartTypeBarStacked
cht.SetData c.chDimSeriesNames, c.chDataLiteral,
Session("chartdetail").Item("DS.SeriesName")
cht.SetData c.chDimCategories, c.chDataLiteral,
Session("chartdetail").Item("DS.Categories")

oChart.Charts(0).SeriesCollection(0).Border.Color = c.chColorNone
oChart.Charts(0).SeriesCollection(0).Interior.Color = c.chColorNone
oChart.Charts(0).SeriesCollection(0).SetData
c.chDimValues, c.chDataLiteral, arrStartDate
oChart.Charts(0).SeriesCollection(1).SetData
c.chDimValues, c.chDataLiteral, arrDateDiff

'_____-

'*** X AXIS BOTTOM SECTION ***
'_____-

set ax = cht.Axes(c.chAxisPositionBottom)
ax.HasTitle = True
ax.Title.Caption = "Date"
ax.Title.Font.Name = "arial"
ax.Title.Font.Size = 10
ax.NumberFormat = "Short date"

'_____-

'*** Y AXIS LEFT SECTION *****
'_____-

set ay = cht.Axes(c.chAxisPositionLeft)
oChart.Charts(0).Axes(c.chAxisPositionLeft).Font.Name = "Tahoma"
oChart.Charts(0).Axes(c.chAxisPositionLeft).Font.Size = 7
```

```
'_____

'*** TITLE SECTION **********
'_____

    Dim strTitle
    strTitle = "Nurse Retention Project: Gantt Chart View"
    oChart.Charts(0).HasTitle = True
    cht.Title.Caption = strTitle
    set fnt = oChart.Charts(0).Title.Font
    fnt.Bold = True

'_____

'*** LEGEND SECTION **********
'_____

    oChart.Charts(0).HasLegend = False

'_____

'*** PLOT SECTION **********
'_____

    cht.PlotArea.Interior.Color = "#CCCC99"

'_____

'***** FILES FOR GIF CREATION ****
'_____

    sFname = "GanttChart.gif"
    'binaryfilestream object
    Dim m_objBinaryFile

    Response.Expires = -1
    Response.ContentType = "image/gif"
    sFullFileName = Server.MapPath(".") & "\" & sFname
    oChart.ExportPicture sFullFileName, "gif", 750, 400
```

```
on error resume next

set m_objBinaryFile =
server.CreateObject("BinaryFileStream.Object")
Response.BinaryWrite
m_objBinaryFile.GetFileBytes(CStr(sFullFileName))

Response.Write "<img src='" & sFname & "'>"

m_objBinaryFile.DeleteFile CStr(sFullFileName)

m_objBinaryFile.Close
set m_objBinaryFile = nothing

Response.Flush

'Clear the chart object
oChart.Close
Set oChart = nothing
c.close
set c = nothing
%>
</body>
</html>
```

XY Scatter Chart

Scatter Line Chart

An XY (scatter) chart either shows the relationships among the numeric values in several data series or plots two groups of numbers as one of XY coordinates. The XY Scatter chart usually shows uneven intervals–or clusters–of data and is commonly used for scientific data.

In the following table, Time is our X values, and volume, average volume, and predicted volume.

Table 3.8: Scatter Chart Table

Time	Volume	Average_Volume	Predicted_Volume
1	325	280	300
2	332	260	300
3	288	180	250
4	362	190	350
5	378	325	350
6	482	400	450
7	598	425	550
8	780	500	850

Get data from the database

```
<%
Dim oChart, c, Time(), Volume(), Average_Volume(),
Predicted_Volume(), lngCounter
ReDim Time(0)
ReDim Volume(0)
ReDim Average_Volume(0)
ReDim Predicted_Volume(0)
lngCounter = 0

'Loop through the record set

Do While Not rsResults1.EOF
   ReDim Preserve Time(lngCounter)
   ReDim Preserve Volume(lngCounter)
   ReDim Preserve Average_Volume(lngCounter)
   ReDim Preserve Predicted_Volume(lngCounter)
   Time(lngCounter) = CStr(rsResults1("Time"))
   Volume(lngCounter) = rsResults1("Volume")
   Average_Volume(lngCounter) = rsResults1("Average_Volume")
   Predicted_Volume(lngCounter) = rsResults1("Predicted_Volume")
   lngCounter = lngCounter + 1
   rsResults1.MoveNext
Loop
%>
```

Declare chart type:

```
<%
' Create a Chart Object
Set oChart = Server.CreateObject("OWC.Chart")
Set c = oChart.Constants

oChart.Border.Color = c.chColorNone
oChart.Charts.Add
oChart.Charts(0).Type                                    =
oChart.Constants.chChartTypeScatterMarkers
%>
```

In order to create a scatter chart, each series must have X values and Y values for every point. Therefore, we declare the data values as follows:

```
<%
oChart.Charts(0).SeriesCollection.Add
oChart.Charts(0).SeriesCollection(0).Border.Color = "black"
'Add series values
oChart.Charts(0).SeriesCollection(0).SetData c.chDimXValues,
c.chDataLiteral, Time
oChart.Charts(0).SeriesCollection(0).SetData c.chDimYValues,
c.chDataLiteral, Volume
oChart.Charts(0).SeriesCollection.Add
oChart.Charts(0).SeriesCollection(1).SetData c.chDimXValues,
c.chDataLiteral, Time
oChart.Charts(0).SeriesCollection(1).SetData c.chDimYValues,
c.chDataLiteral, Average_Volume
oChart.Charts(0).SeriesCollection.Add
oChart.Charts(0).SeriesCollection(2).SetData c.chDimXValues,
c.chDataLiteral, Time
oChart.Charts(0).SeriesCollection(2).SetData c.chDimYValues,
c.chDataLiteral, Predicted_Volume
'Add series titles
oChart.Charts(0).SeriesCollection(0).Caption = "Volume"
```

```
oChart.Charts(0).SeriesCollection(1).Caption = "Average Volume"
oChart.Charts(0).SeriesCollection(2).Caption = "Predicted Volume"
%>
```

The whole code section looks like this:

```
<%@ language="vbscript" %>
<% Option Explicit %>

<html>
<body>

<Table align="left" width="100%">
<%
Dim    oChart,    c,    Time(),    Volume(),    Average_Volume(),
Predicted_Volume(), lngCounter
Dim fnt, sFname
Dim oConn, rsResults1, strSQL, strConn
set oConn=Server.CreateObject("ADODB.connection")
set rsResults1=Server.CreateObject("ADODB.recordset")

strConn = "driver=SQL Server;server=YourServer;"
strConn = strConn & "database=YourDatabase;uid=YourUserID;
pwd=YourPassword;"

oConn.ConnectionString = strConn
oConn.Open

strSQL = "SELECT * FROM Scatter"

'Open recordset using SQL string above

rsResults.Open strSQL, oConn

ReDim Time(0)
ReDim Volume(0)
ReDim Average_Volume(0)
ReDim Predicted_Volume(0)
lngCounter = 0
```

```
'Loop through the record set
Do While Not rsResults1.EOF
   ReDim Preserve Time(lngCounter)
   ReDim Preserve Volume(lngCounter)
   ReDim Preserve Average_Volume(lngCounter)
   ReDim Preserve Predicted_Volume(lngCounter)
   Time(lngCounter) = CStr(rsResults1("Time"))
   Volume(lngCounter) = rsResults1("Volume")
   Average_Volume(lngCounter) = rsResults1("Average_Volume")
   Predicted_Volume(lngCounter) = rsResults1("Predicted_Volume")
   lngCounter = lngCounter + 1
   rsResults1.MoveNext
Loop

'Cleanup the record set
rsResults1.Close
Set rsResults1 = Nothing
oConn.Close
Set oConn = Nothing

' Create a Chart Object
Set oChart = Server.CreateObject("OWC.Chart")
Set c = oChart.Constants

oChart.Border.Color = c.chColorNone

oChart.Charts.Add

oChart.Charts(0).Type =
oChart.Constants.chChartTypeScatterLineMarkers

oChart.Charts(0).SeriesCollection.Add
oChart.Charts(0).SeriesCollection(0).Border.Color = "black"
'Add series values
oChart.Charts(0).SeriesCollection(0).SetData c.chDimXValues,
c.chDataLiteral, Time
```

```
oChart.Charts(0).SeriesCollection(0).SetData c.chDimYValues,
c.chDataLiteral, Volume
oChart.Charts(0).SeriesCollection.Add
oChart.Charts(0).SeriesCollection(1).SetData c.chDimXValues,
c.chDataLiteral, Time
oChart.Charts(0).SeriesCollection(1).SetData c.chDimYValues,
c.chDataLiteral, Average_Volume
oChart.Charts(0).SeriesCollection.Add
oChart.Charts(0).SeriesCollection(2).SetData c.chDimXValues,
c.chDataLiteral, Time
oChart.Charts(0).SeriesCollection(2).SetData c.chDimYValues,
c.chDataLiteral, Predicted_Volume
'Add series titles
oChart.Charts(0).SeriesCollection(0).Caption = "Volume"
oChart.Charts(0).SeriesCollection(1).Caption = "Average Volume"
oChart.Charts(0).SeriesCollection(2).Caption = "Predicted Volume"
'Format title
oChart.Charts(0).HasTitle = True
oChart.Charts(0).Title.Caption = "Call Volume on New Year's Eve"
   set fnt = oChart.Charts(0).Title.Font
   fnt.Name = "arial"
   fnt.Size = 14
   fnt.Bold = True
'Format legend font and position
oChart.Charts(0).PlotArea.Interior.Color = "#CCCC99"
oChart.Charts(0).HasLegend = True
oChart.Charts(0).Legend.Position = c.chLegendPositionBottom
oChart.Charts(0).Legend.Font = "Tahoma"
oChart.Charts(0).Legend.Font.size = 7
oChart.Charts(0).Legend.LegendEntries(0).Visible = True

'Create a graph and specify the graph size
sFname = "Tempchart.gif"
oChart.ExportPicture server.MapPath(sFname), "gif", 400, 400
```

```
' Create a link to the generated file
Response.Write "<tr><td><img align='top' src='" & sFname &
"'></td></tr></table>"
%>
</body>
</html>
```

This above code will produce the following chart on the web page:

Figure 3.18: Scatter Line Chart with Markers

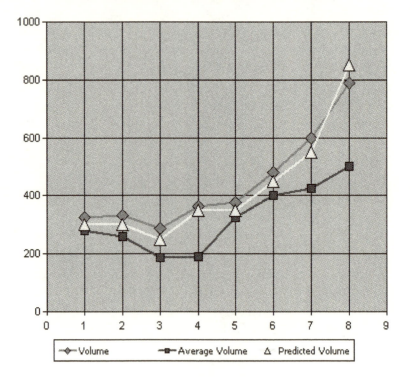

Scatter Smooth Line Chart

To change the type XY scatter smooth line chart, simply change the chart type constant to the chart type to smooth line:

```
<%
oChart.Charts(0).Type =
oChart.Constants.chChartTypeScatterSmoothLine
%>
```

With all other code remains the same, this will produce the following output:

Figure 3.19: Scatter Smooth Line Chart

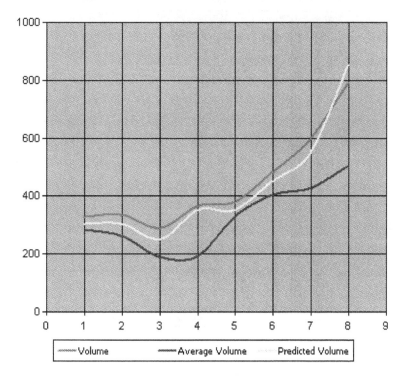

Scatter Line Chart

To change the type XY scatter line chart, simply change the chart type constant to the chart type to scatter line:

```
<%
oChart.Charts(0).Type = oChart.Constants.chChartTypeScatterLine
%>
```

With all other code remains the same, this will produce the following output:

Figure 3.20: Scatter Line Chart

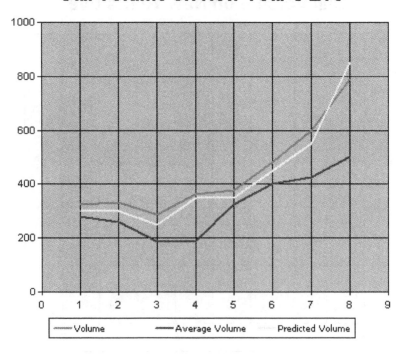

Scatter Smooth Line Chart with Markers

To change the type XY scatter smooth line chart with markers, simply change the chart type constant to the chart type to the following:

```
<%
oChart.Charts(0).Type =
oChart.Constants.chChartTypeScatterSmoothLineMarkers
%>
```

With all other code remains the same, this will produce the following output:

Figure 3.21: Scatter Smooth Line Chart with Markers

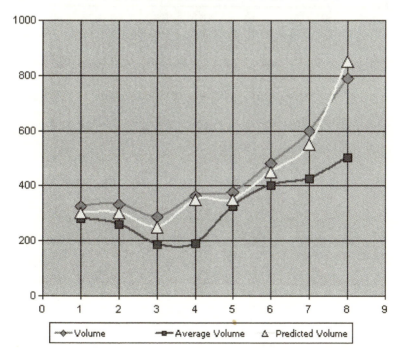

Scatter Chart with Markers

To change the type XY scatter chart with markers, simply change the chart type constant to the chart type to the following:

```
<%
oChart.Charts(0).Type = oChart.Constants.chChartTypeScatterMarkers
%>
```

With all other code remains the same, this will produce the following output:

Figure 3.22: Scatter Line Chart

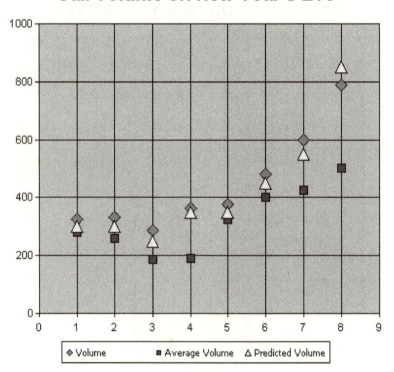

Scatter Chart with Line Filled

To change the type XY scatter chart with line filled, simply change the chart type constant to the chart type to the following:

```
<%
oChart.Charts(0).Type =
oChart.Constants.chChartTypeScatterLineFilled
%>
```

With all other code remains the same, this will produce the following output:

Figure 3.23: Scatter Line Chart

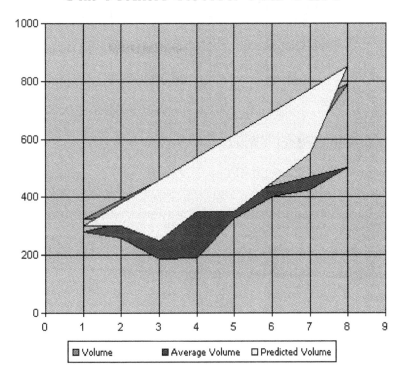

Stock Chart

Stock charts are gaining more popularity on the web pages than ever due to the booming of online trading and some other reasons. There are two types of stock charts: high-low-close and open-high-low-close. Stock chart can also be used for data that not related to stock exchange. For example, we can use high-low-close chart to indicate the high-low-average selling price of houses in the same neighborhood for home appraisal analysis, etc.

Our stock prices for the dates between 6/1/00 to 6/4/00 are in the following table:

Table 3.9: Stock Chart Table

Trading_Date	High	Low	Open_Price	Close_Price
6/1/00	12.35	10.58	9.08	9.98
6/2/00	11.82	8.02	9	10.05
6/3/00	11.75	11.13	11.06	11.5
6/4/00	12.25	11.08	10.25	12.1

High-Low-Close Stock Chart

High-Low-Close Stock chart has four series of data: trading date as categories on X axis, high, low, and close prices for Y axis. Accordingly, you should declare and retrieve those four series of data from the database table.

First we declare the four arrays we need. Then ReDim and Preserve them during the database record set loop through.

```
<%
Dim Trading_Date(), High(), Low(), Close_Price()
ReDim Trading_Date(0)
ReDim High(0)
```

```
ReDim Low(0)
ReDim Close_Price(0)
lngCounter = 0

'Loop through the record set

Do While Not rsResults1.EOF
   ReDim Preserve Trading_Date(lngCounter)
   ReDim Preserve High(lngCounter)
   ReDim Preserve Low(lngCounter)
   ReDim Preserve Close_Price(lngCounter)
   Trading_Date(lngCounter) = CStr(rsResults1("Trading_Date"))
   High(lngCounter) = rsResults1("High")
   Low(lngCounter) = rsResults1("Low")
   Close_Price(lngCounter) = rsResults1("Close_Price")
   lngCounter = lngCounter + 1
   rsResults1.MoveNext
Loop
%>
```

Then we need to assign our values into the chart series accordingly:

```
<%
'Add series values
oChart.Charts(0).SeriesCollection(0).SetData c.chDimCategories,
c.chDataLiteral, Trading_Date
oChart.Charts(0).SeriesCollection(0).SetData c.chDimHighValues,
c.chDataLiteral, High
oChart.Charts(0).SeriesCollection(0).SetData c.chDimLowValues,
c.chDataLiteral, Low
oChart.Charts(0).SeriesCollection(0).SetData c.chDimCloseValues,
c.chDataLiteral, Close_Price
%>
```

Figure 3.23: High-Low-Close Stock Chart

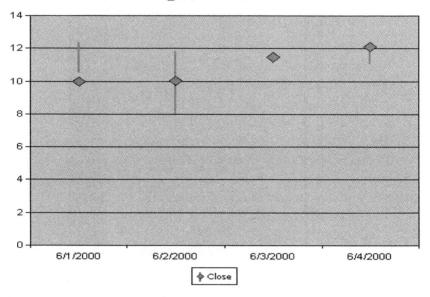

The following code sample is used to create the chart as above:

```
<%@ language="vbscript" %>
<% Option Explicit %>

<html>
<body>
<Table align="left" width="100%">

<%
Dim oChart, c, Trading_Date(), High(), Low(), Close_Price(),
lngCounter Dim fnt, sFname
Dim oConn, rsResults1, strSQL, strConn

set oConn=Server.CreateObject("ADODB.connection")
set rsResults1=Server.CreateObject("ADODB.recordset")
```

```
strConn = "driver=SQL Server;server=YourServer;"
strConn = strConn & "database=YourDatabase;uid=YourUserID;
pwd=YourPassword;"

oConn.ConnectionString = strConn
oConn.Open

sSQL = "SELECT * FROM Stock"

rsResults1.Open strSQL, oConn

ReDim Trading_Date(0)
ReDim High(0)
ReDim Low(0)
ReDim Close_Price(0)
lngCounter = 0

'Loop through the record set

Do While Not rsResults1.EOF
   ReDim Preserve Trading_Date(lngCounter)
   ReDim Preserve High(lngCounter)
   ReDim Preserve Low(lngCounter)
   ReDim Preserve Close_Price(lngCounter)
   Trading_Date(lngCounter) = CStr(rsResults1("Trading_Date"))
   High(lngCounter) = rsResults1("High")
   Low(lngCounter) = rsResults1("Low")
   Close_Price(lngCounter) = rsResults1("Close_Price")
   lngCounter = lngCounter + 1
   rsResults1.MoveNext
Loop

'Cleanup the record set
rsResults1.Close
Set rsResults1 = Nothing
oABCData1.CloseABCConnection oABCConn1
Set oABCData1 = Nothing
```

```
' Create a Chart Object
Set oChart = Server.CreateObject("OWC.Chart")
Set c = oChart.Constants

oChart.Border.Color = c.chColorNone

oChart.Charts.Add

oChart.Charts(0).Type = oChart.Constants.chChartTypeStockHLC

oChart.Charts(0).SeriesCollection.Add
oChart.Charts(0).SeriesCollection(0).Border.Color = "black"
'Add series values
oChart.Charts(0).SeriesCollection(0).SetData c.chDimCategories,
c.chDataLiteral, Trading_Date
oChart.Charts(0).SeriesCollection(0).SetData c.chDimHighValues,
c.chDataLiteral, High
oChart.Charts(0).SeriesCollection(0).SetData c.chDimLowValues,
c.chDataLiteral, Low
oChart.Charts(0).SeriesCollection(0).SetData c.chDimCloseValues,
c.chDataLiteral, Close_Price
'Add series titles
oChart.Charts(0).SeriesCollection(0).Caption = "Close"
'Format title
oChart.Charts(0).HasTitle = True
oChart.Charts(0).Title.Caption = "Stock: High, Low, and Close"
   set fnt = oChart.Charts(0).Title.Font
   fnt.Name = "arial"
   fnt.Size = 14
   fnt.Bold = True
'Format legend font and position
oChart.Charts(0).PlotArea.Interior.Color = "#CCCC99"
oChart.Charts(0).HasLegend = True
oChart.Charts(0).Legend.Position = c.chLegendPositionBottom
oChart.Charts(0).Legend.Font = "Tahoma"
oChart.Charts(0).Legend.Font.size = 7
oChart.Charts(0).Legend.LegendEntries(0).Visible = True
```

```
'Create a graph and specify the graph size
sFname = "Tempchart.gif"
oChart.ExportPicture server.MapPath(sFname), "gif", 400, 400

' Create a link to the generated file
Response.Write "<tr><td><img align='top' src='" & sFname &
"'></td></tr></table>"

%>

</body>
</html>
```

Open-High-Low-Close Stock Chart

Once you created the High-Low-Close stock chart, the Open-High-Low-Close chart is just one step away: add open series into the code. You start with Dim, Redim, and Preserve procedure as usual, and assign open prices into the array:

```
<%
Dim Trading_Date(), High(), Low(), Open_Price(), Close_Price()

ReDim Trading_Date(0)
ReDim High(0)
ReDim Low(0)
ReDim Open_Price(0)
ReDim Close_Price(0)
lngCounter = 0

'Loop through the record set

Do While Not rsResults1.EOF
   ReDim Preserve Trading_Date(lngCounter)
   ReDim Preserve High(lngCounter)
   ReDim Preserve Low(lngCounter)
   ReDim Preserve Open_Price(lngCounter)
   ReDim Preserve Close_Price(lngCounter)
```

```
      Trading_Date(lngCounter) = CStr(rsResults1("Trading_Date"))
      High(lngCounter) = rsResults1("High")
      Low(lngCounter) = rsResults1("Low")
      Open_Price(lngCounter) = rsResults1("Open_Price")
      Close_Price(lngCounter) = rsResults1("Close_Price")
      lngCounter = lngCounter + 1
      rsResults1.MoveNext
   Loop
   %>
```

Finally change the chart type into Open-High-Low-Close stock chart: and add the Open array to the open price series collection:

```
<%
oChart.Charts.Add

oChart.Charts(0).Type = oChart.Constants.chChartTypeStockOHLC

oChart.Charts(0).SeriesCollection.Add
oChart.Charts(0).SeriesCollection(0).Border.Color = "black"

'Add series values
oChart.Charts(0).SeriesCollection(0).SetData c.chDimCategories,
c.chDataLiteral, Trading_Date
oChart.Charts(0).SeriesCollection(0).SetData c.chDimHighValues,
c.chDataLiteral, High
oChart.Charts(0).SeriesCollection(0).SetData c.chDimLowValues,
c.chDataLiteral, Low
oChart.Charts(0).SeriesCollection(0).SetData c.chDimOpenValues,
c.chDataLiteral, Open_Price
oChart.Charts(0).SeriesCollection(0).SetData c.chDimCloseValues,
c.chDataLiteral, Close_Price
%>
```

The Open-High-Low-Close stock chart looks as below:

Figure 3.23: High-Low-Close Stock Chart

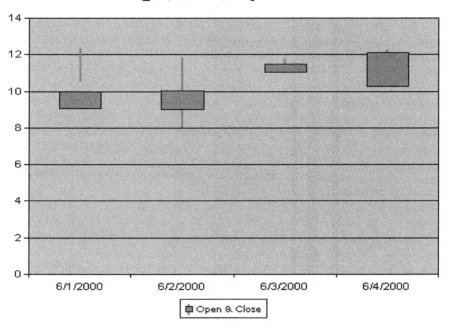

Stock: High, Low, Open and Close

Doughnut Chart

Doughnut chart is similar to pie chart that shows the relationship of parts to a whole. However, doughnut chart can display multiple series of data. Pie chart can only display one series of data. Therefore, it is easier to use doughnut chart when you want to compare the difference between different data series. Each ring of the doughnut represents a separate data series.

Regular Doughnut Chart

To create a regular doughnut chart, we create three series: one for category, one for first data series, one for second data series. Then we declare the chart type as doughnut and add those arrays into the chart series collections:

```
<%
oChart.Charts(0).Type = oChart.Constants.chChartTypeDoughnut

oChart.Charts(0).SeriesCollection.Add
oChart.Charts(0).SeriesCollection(0).SetData c.chDimCategories,
c.chDataLiteral, Categories oChart.Charts(0).SeriesCollection.Add
oChart.Charts(0).SeriesCollection(1).SetData c.chDimValues,
c.chDataLiteral, FirstDoughnutValues
oChart.Charts(0).SeriesCollection.Add
oChart.Charts(0).SeriesCollection(2).SetData c.chDimValues,
c.chDataLiteral, SecondDoughnutValues
%>
```

Figure 3.24: Doughnut Chart

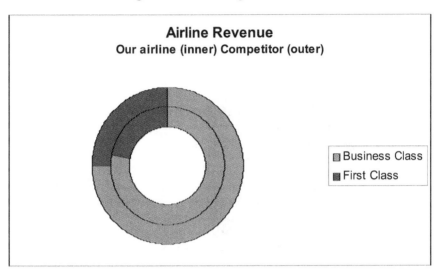

Exploded Doughnut Chart

To create a exploded doughnut chart, we just have to change the chart type into exploded doughnut chart type:

```
<%
oChart.Charts(0).Type =
oChart.Constants.chChartTypeDoughnutExploded
%>
```

Figure 3.25: Exploded Doughnut Chart

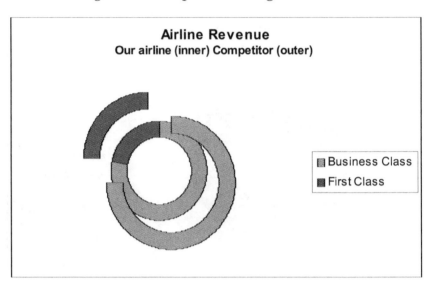

Radar Chart

Radar chart is similar to doughnut chart in terms of coding. To create a two-series radar chart, you just change the chart type to radar type. Each category in the radar chart has its own axis that radiates from the center point. Lines connect all the values in the same series. Therefore, radar chart compares the aggregate values of different data series. The following radar chart compares the government employees' transportation means: by public transportation or by private transportation.

Radar Chart with Line and Markers

Simply declare the chart type as:

```
<%
oChart.Charts(0).Type =
oChart.Constants.chChartTypeRadarLineMarkers
%>
```

Figure 3.25: Radar Chart with Line and Markers

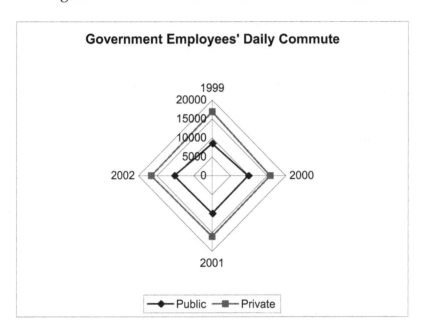

Radar Chart with Line

Simply declare the chart type as:

```
<%
oChart.Charts(0).Type =
oChart.Constants.chChartTypeRadarLine
%>
```

Radar Chart with Smooth Line and Markers

Simply declare the chart type as:

```
<%
oChart.Charts(0).Type =
oChart.Constants.chChartTypeRadarSmoothLineMarkers
%>
```

Radar Chart with Smooth Line

Simply declare the chart type as:

```
<%
oChart.Charts(0).Type =
oChart.Constants.chChartTypeRadarSmoothLine
%>
```

Bubble Chart

A bubble chart is kind of like XY Scatter chart with data marker indicates the value of a third series. If we have the following table of values, number of stores is X axis values, sales is Y axis values, market share is bubble size:

Table 3.10: Bubble Chart Data

Number of Stores	Sales	Market Shares
15	168000	12
25	299000	20
32	379000	26

In order to create a bubble chart, we assign data into three arrays as usual: XValues, YValues, BubbleSize. Then we have to put the arrays into the X axis, Y axis, and Bubble values accordingly:

```
<%
oChart.Charts(0).SeriesCollection(0).SetData c.chDimXValues,
c.chDataLiteral, XValues
oChart.Charts(0).SeriesCollection(0).SetData c.chDimYValues,
c.chDataLiteral, YValues
oChart.Charts(0).SeriesCollection(0).SetData c.chDimBubbleValues,
c.chDataLiteral, BubbleSize
%>
```

We declare the chart type as bubble chart:

```
<%
oChart.Charts(0).Type = oChart.Constants.chChartTypeBubble
%>
```

Our bubble chart will looks like this:

Figure 3.25: Bubble Chart

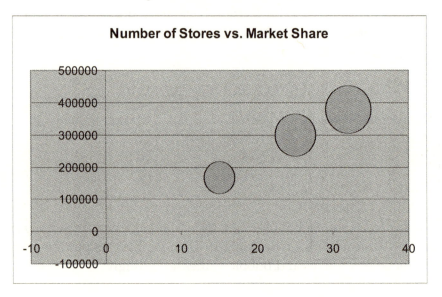

Polar Chart

A polar chart compares the relationship of angles and distances. If we have the following table with degree and frequency information for microphone, we can construct a polar chart from it.

Table 3.11: Polar Chart Data

Degree	Frequency
0	50
30	48
60	45
90	32
120	45
150	48
180	50
210	48
240	45
270	32
300	45
330	48
360	50

To create a polar chart, we first need to declare the polar chart as Polar Smooth Line type. Then add values into the RValues and add degrees into ThetaValues:

```
<%
oChart.Charts(0).Type =
oChart.Constants.chChartTypePolarSmoothLine

oChart.Charts(0).SeriesCollection.Add
oChart.Charts(0).SeriesCollection(0).Border.Color = "black"
'Add series values
```

```
oChart.Charts(0).SeriesCollection(0).SetData c.chDimRValues,
c.chDataLiteral, Frequency
oChart.Charts(0).SeriesCollection(0).SetData c.chDimThetaValues,
c.chDataLiteral, Degree
oChart.Charts(0).SeriesCollection(0).Caption = "Frequency"
%>
```

Figure 3.26: Polar Chart with Smooth Line

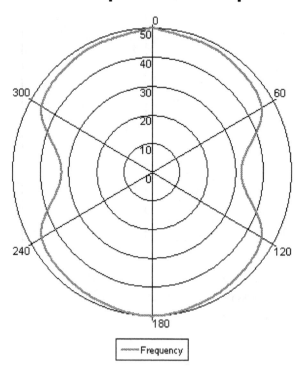

Combination Chart

A combination chart uses two or more chart types to emphasize that the chart contains different kinds of information. To create a combination chart, we have to set each individual series into the chart type you desire. Please note that not all chart types can be combined. The OWC chart component only allows you to combine Column, Line, and Area chart types together. If you attempt to change a series on a chart to an incompatible chart type, all series types on the chart are changed. In other words, you have changed the Type property of the chart object itself.

Both charts and series have Type property. Each individual series has a type, and if all series in a chart happen to have the same type, the Chart object's Type property returns that type. Setting the Type property of a Chart object changes the chart type for every series in the chart. Note that if you query the Type property of a combination chart, the returned value is chChartTypeCombo (or-1). chChartTypeCombo indicates that the series on the chart has different types. You cannot set a chart Type to chChartTypeCombo; if you do, you receive an error.

The following figure shows a combination chart of line chart with markers and column chart, this type of combination chart is used most often.

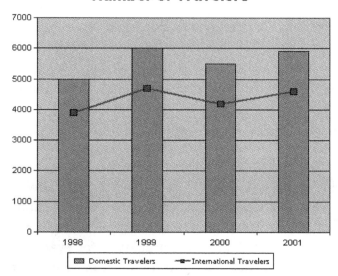

The code sample to create the chart above is follows:

```
<%@ language="vbscript" %>
<% Option Explicit %>
<html>
<body>

<Table align="left" width="100%">
<%
    Dim oChart, c, ch, fnt, sFname

    'Create a Chart Object
    Set oChart = Server.CreateObject("OWC.Chart")
    Set c = oChart.Constants

    oChart.Border.Color = c.chColorNone
```

```
'Create a new chart in the chart space
oChart.Charts.Add
Set ch = oChart.Charts(0)

'Add a second series of clustered column chart
Dim oSeries1
Set oSeries1 = ch.SeriesCollection.Add
With oSeries1
        .Caption = "Domestic Travelers"
        .SetData c.chDimCategories, c.chDataLiteral, _
              Array("1998", "1999", "2000", "2001")
        .SetData c.chDimValues, c.chDataLiteral, _
              Array(5000, 6000, 5500, 5900)
        .Type = c.chChartTypeColumnClustered
End With

'Add a second series of Line with markers chart
Dim oSeries2
Set oSeries2 = ch.SeriesCollection.Add
With oSeries2
        .Caption = "International Travelers"
        .SetData c.chDimCategories, c.chDataLiteral, _
              Array("1998", "1999", "2000", "2001")
        .SetData c.chDimValues, c.chDataLiteral, _
              Array(3900, 4700, 4200, 4600)
        .Type = c.chChartTypeLineMarkers
End With

'Format title caption and font attributes
ch.HasTitle = True
ch.Title.Caption = "Number of Travelers"
        set fnt = ch.Title.Font
        fnt.Name = "arial"
        fnt.Size = 14
        fnt.Bold = True
```

```
'Format legend font and position attributes

ch.PlotArea.Interior.Color = "#CCCC99"
ch.HasLegend = True
ch.Legend.Position = c.chLegendPositionBottom
ch.Legend.Font = "Tahoma"
ch.Legend.Font.size = 7
ch.Legend.LegendEntries(0).Visible = True

'Create a graph and specify the graph size
sFname = "Tempchart.gif"
oChart.ExportPicture server.MapPath(sFname), "gif", 400, 400

'Create a link to the generated file
Response.Write "<tr><td><img align='top' src='" & sFname
Response.Write "'></td></tr></table>"
%>
</body>
</html>
```

Sometimes we need to add another axis on the right for the combination chart. To add another axis, simply add the following code above format title section and below the last End With.

```
<%
'Add the second value axis to the chart
ch.Axes.Add ch.Scalings(c.chDimValues), _
    c.chAxisPositionRight, c.chValueAxis
%>
```

The chart will looks like this:

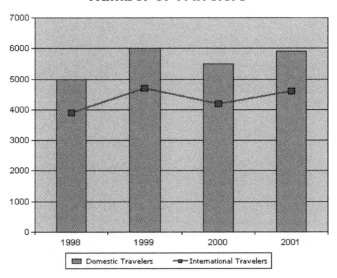

A combination chart can have two value axes. The Value axes on a chart always have the same scale. In a scenario where you have two series where the y-values are considerably different in value, the Series with the smaller values may look "dwarfed" by the Series with the larger values. Unfortunately, when using the OWC Chart component there is no way to avoid this behavior because the value axes cannot have different scales.

You might consider create two separate charts in the ChartSpace for using two series with very different values as an alternative. The following two charts come from the same chart space with different scales:

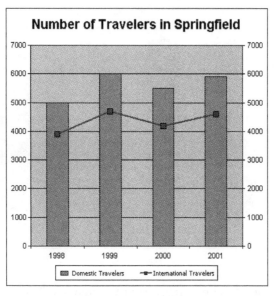

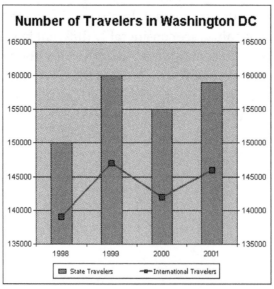

Create Multiple Charts in the Same Chart Space

We can create multiple charts in the same chart space. The following code sample is used to create two charts in the same chart space:

```
<%@ language="vbscript" %>
<% Option Explicit %>
<html>
<body>

<Table align="left" width="100%">
<%
    Dim oChart, c, ch, fnt, sFname

    'Create a Chart Object
    Set oChart = Server.CreateObject("OWC.Chart")
    Set c = oChart.Constants

    oChart.Border.Color = c.chColorNone

    'Create a new chart in the chart space
    oChart.Clear

    oChart.Charts.Add
    Set ch = oChart.Charts(0)

    'Add a second series of clustered column chart
    Dim oSeries1
    Set oSeries1 = ch.SeriesCollection.Add
    With oSeries1
            .Caption = "Domestic Travelers"
            .SetData c.chDimCategories, c.chDataLiteral, _
                Array("1998", "1999", "2000", "2001")
            .SetData c.chDimValues, c.chDataLiteral, _
                Array(5000, 6000, 5500, 5900)
            .Type = c.chChartTypeColumnClustered
    End With
```

```
'Add a second series of Line with markers chart
Dim oSeries2
Set oSeries2 = ch.SeriesCollection.Add
With oSeries2
      .Caption = "International Travelers"
      .SetData c.chDimCategories, c.chDataLiteral, _
            Array("1998", "1999", "2000", "2001")
      .SetData c.chDimValues, c.chDataLiteral, _
            Array(3900, 4700, 4200, 4600)
      .Type = c.chChartTypeLineMarkers
End With

'Add the second value axis to the chart
ch.Axes.Add ch.Scalings(c.chDimValues), _
      c.chAxisPositionRight, c.chValueAxis

'Format title caption and font attributes
ch.HasTitle = True
ch.Title.Caption = "Number of Travelers in Springfield"
      set fnt = ch.Title.Font
      fnt.Name = "arial"
      fnt.Size = 14
      fnt.Bold = True

'Format legend font and position attributes

ch.PlotArea.Interior.Color = "#CCCC99"
ch.HasLegend = True
ch.Legend.Position = c.chLegendPositionBottom
ch.Legend.Font = "Tahoma"
ch.Legend.Font.size = 7
ch.Legend.LegendEntries(0).Visible = True

'Create a graph and specify the graph size
sFname = "Tempchart.gif"
oChart.ExportPicture server.MapPath(sFname), "gif", 400, 400
```

```
'Create a link to the generated file
Response.Write "<tr><td><img align='top' src='" & sFname &
"'></td>"

'**********************************************************
'Second chart in the same chart space
'**********************************************************

Dim ch1, fnt1, sFname1

'Create another new chart in the chart space
oChart.Clear
oChart.Charts.Add
Set ch1 = oChart.Charts(0)

'Add a second series of clustered column chart
Dim oSeries11
Set oSeries11 = ch1.SeriesCollection.Add
With oSeries11
        .Caption = "Domestic Travelers"
        .SetData c.chDimCategories, c.chDataLiteral, _
            Array("1998", "1999", "2000", "2001")
        .SetData c.chDimValues, c.chDataLiteral, _
            Array(150000, 160000, 155000, 159000)
        .Type = c.chChartTypeColumnClustered
End With

'Add a second series of Line with markers chart
Dim oSeries21
Set oSeries21 = ch1.SeriesCollection.Add
With oSeries21
        .Caption = "International Travelers"
        .SetData c.chDimCategories, c.chDataLiteral, _
            Array("1998", "1999", "2000", "2001")
        .SetData c.chDimValues, c.chDataLiteral, _
            Array(139000, 147000, 142000, 146000)
        .Type = c.chChartTypeLineMarkers
End With
```

```
'Add the second value axis to the chart
ch1.Axes.Add ch1.Scalings(c.chDimValues), _
        c.chAxisPositionRight, c.chValueAxis

'Format title caption and font attributes
ch1.HasTitle = True
ch1.Title.Caption = "Number of Travelers in Washington DC"
        set fnt1 = ch1.Title.Font
        fnt1.Name = "arial"
        fnt1.Size = 14
        fnt1.Bold = True

'Format legend font and position attributes

ch1.PlotArea.Interior.Color = "#CCCC99"
ch1.HasLegend = True
ch1.Legend.Position = c.chLegendPositionBottom
ch1.Legend.Font = "Tahoma"
ch1.Legend.Font.size = 7
ch1.Legend.LegendEntries(1).Visible = True

'Create a graph and specify the graph size
sFname1 = "Tempchart2.gif"
oChart.ExportPicture server.MapPath(sFname1), "gif", 400, 400

'Create a link to the generated file
Response.Write "<td><img align='top' src='" & sFname1 &
"'></td></tr></table>"

%>
</body>
</html>
```

The above code will create multiple charts in the same chart space. Sometimes it is necessary to create multiple charts in the same chart space.

Summary

In this chapter we covered all different chart types and provided code sample for every one of them. We also added Gantt chart code sample into the chapter although it is only a mutation of column chart type. But it is a useful chart type of project management purposes.

In Office XP Office Web components, three-dimensional charts available. To create three-dimensional charts simply add 3D inside the chart type statement. Please note not all chart types have three-dimensional charts available.

Chapter 4

Advanced Charting Techniques

In this chapter we will take a look at some advanced charting techniques that will be useful in addition to the basic charting techniques covered by the previous chapter. We will introduce how to code split axis, add data labels, etc. We will also compare the differences of two chart creating methods: creating chart as an object vs. creating chart as a bitmap image. In the very last section, we will cover some knowledge regarding charting with XML data.

Split Axis

In order to show small and large numbers on the same axis and still show the local variation, you need to split a value axis at a certain point. You can have one split per value axis. To split the axis you need to set the HasSplit property of the axis's Scaling object to True and then setting the SplitMinimum and SplitMaximum properties to the values you want to split.

If we have three major air pollutants we are concerned with: nitrogen dioxide, sulfur dioxide, and carbon monxide.

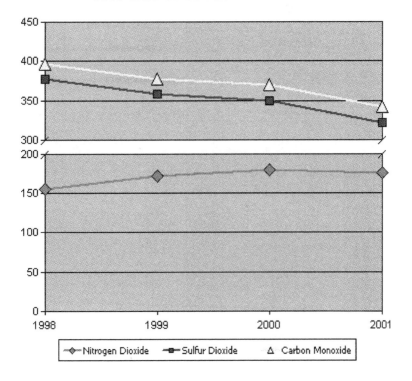

The Level of Air Pollutants

The following code sample shows how to split axis:

```
<%
oChart.Charts(0).SeriesCollection(0).Caption = "Nitrogen Dioxide"
oChart.Charts(0).SeriesCollection(1).Caption = "Sulfur Dioxide"
oChart.Charts(0).SeriesCollection(2).Caption = "Carbon Monoxide"
'Format title
oChart.Charts(0).HasTitle = True
oChart.Charts(0).Title.Caption = "The Level of Air Pollutants"
    set fnt = oChart.Charts(0).Title.Font
    fnt.Name = "arial"
    fnt.Size = 14
    fnt.Bold = True
'Format legend font and position
oChart.Charts(0).PlotArea.Interior.Color = "#CCCC99"
oChart.Charts(0).HasLegend = True
oChart.Charts(0).Legend.Position = c.chLegendPositionBottom
oChart.Charts(0).Legend.Font = "Tahoma"
oChart.Charts(0).Legend.Font.size = 7
oChart.Charts(0).Legend.LegendEntries(0).Visible = True
Dim ax
Set ax = oChart.Charts(0).Axes(0)
ax.Scaling.HasSplit = True
ax.Scaling.SplitMaximum = 300
ax.Scaling.SplitMinimum = 200
%>
```

Add Data Labels

Every chart must provide useful data to its user. Data labels are great tools to give user accurate values on the chart. Simple chart types such as pie chart, data label is almost always necessary to ensure the chart is informative. The following chart is unacceptable—neither does it tells the user how much each hour air pollutant is nor does it has correct and descriptive legend. This type of chart is simply not useful to users. Worst of all, the chart type is wrong for the type of data that needs to be presented.

The Level of Air Pollutants

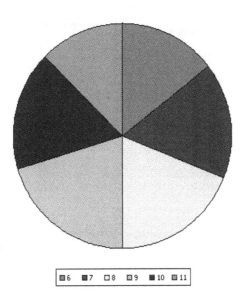

To improve the chart, we need to add data label for each series and improve the chart type and legend presentation. So the improved chart looks like this one:

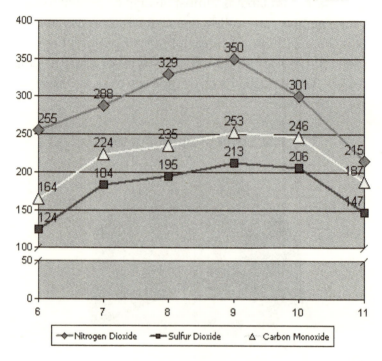

To add data labels to each series, simple follow this syntax:

```
<%
'Add data label for the first series
oChart.Charts(0).SeriesCollection(0).DataLabelsCollection.Add
'Add data label for the second series
oChart.Charts(0).SeriesCollection(1).DataLabelsCollection.Add
'Add data label for the third series
oChart.Charts(0).SeriesCollection(2).DataLabelsCollection.
Add
%>
```

Create Chart Methods

There are two ways to create a chart on the web page using OWC Chart Component: create the chart as an object and create the chart as a bitmap image. We will look at how to create charts using different methods and compare the differences between the two types of charts.

Create chart as an object

To create chart as an object, we must include the object id, class id, and style. In the style section, you can specify the width and height of the chart object according to your chart. Then put the chart object into OnLoad function so the object will load automatically when the page is retrieved by web users. Here is an example:

```
<html>
<body>

<object   id=ChartSpace1   classid=CLSID:0002E500-0000-0000-
C000-000000000046 style="width:100%;height:350"></object>

<script language=vbscript>

Sub Window_OnLoad()

   Dim oChart
   Dim oSeries1, oSeries2
   dim oConst

   'Ensure ChartSpace1 is empty:
   ChartSpace1.Clear

   Set oConst = ChartSpace1.Constants

   'Create a new chart in the ChartSpace
   Set oChart = ChartSpace1.Charts.Add
```

```
'Add a series of type Column
Set oSeries1 = oChart.SeriesCollection.Add
With oSeries1
        .Caption = "Sales"
        .SetData oConst.chDimCategories, oConst.chDataLiteral, _
              Array("1994", "1995", "1996", "1997")
        .SetData oConst.chDimValues, oConst.chDataLiteral, _
              Array(50, 60, 55, 59)
        .Type = oConst.chChartTypeColumnClustered
End With

'Add a second series of type Line
Set oSeries2 = oChart.SeriesCollection.Add
With oSeries2
        .Caption = "Profit"
        .SetData oConst.chDimCategories, oConst.chDataLiteral, _
              Array("1994", "1995", "1996", "1997")
        .SetData oConst.chDimValues, oConst.chDataLiteral, _
              Array(39, 47, 52, 46)
        .Type = oConst.chChartTypeLine
End With

'Add a second value axis to the Chart
oChart.Axes.Add oChart.Scalings(oConst.chDimValues), _
        oConst.chAxisPositionRight, oConst.chValueAxis

'Display the legend
oChart.HasLegend = True
oChart.Legend.Position = oConst.chLegendPositionBottom

'Display the title for the chart
oChart.HasTitle = True
oChart.Title.Caption = "Four Year Overview"

End Sub

</script>
</body>
</html>
```

The above code will produce the following results on the web page:

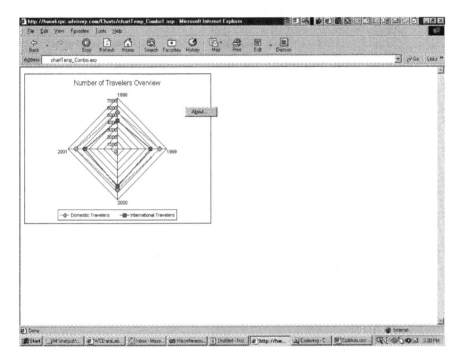

Create Chart as Bitmap Image

All the charts we have created so far are bitmap images. We won't waste time and paper to cover how to create bitmap charts again.

What's difference between the two methods?

When you see the chart on web page created as an object or created as a bitmap image, the chart looks identical. However, when you right click on the image that created as an object, you will see the popup menu has only one item on it "About..." as shown on the above picture. So you can not save this chart to your local drive directly.

But if you right click on the chart that created as a bitmap image, you will see a pop up menu has several items as shown in the following picture. One of the item is "Save As..."–to save the image directly to your local drive directly.

Depending on the purpose of your web site and the chart you created, this may be a significant difference for the users. If users would like to save the chart on their local drives to embed into their Word document, for example, the chart that created as an object will disappoint them. Since they cannot save those charts directly.

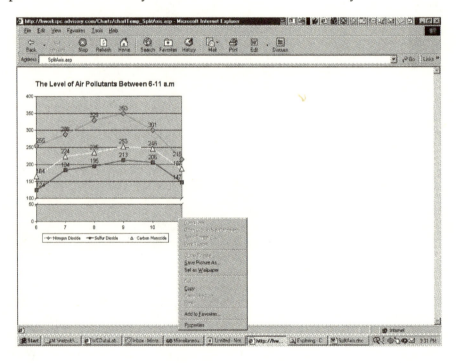

Cleanup Methods

In our previous chapter, we always create the image using a temporary name. Therefore, each time you create and reload the same web page, the newly generate image will replace the previous one. This is OK in many cases but not in all cases. Sometimes you may need to create images and keep them on the server with a unique name for everyone of them. In order to do this, you can use the GetTempName method of the FileSystemObject:

```
<%
Dim temFileName, objFSO
Set objFSO =
Server.CreateObject("Scripting.FileSystemObject")
tmpFileName = strTmpDir &
objFSO.GetBaseName(objFSO.GetTempName) & ".gif"
%>
```

If your web pages have created too many images on the server, you may need to implement some sort of cleanup schema to clean up the files periodically. The following code section allow you to clean up the images on the server that older than 10 minutes. Of course, you can set the value to the number of minutes you desired for periodic cleaning.

```
<%
Sub CleanUpGIF(GIFpath)
   Dim objFS
   Dim objFolder
   Dim gif

   set objFS = Server.CreateObject("Scripting.FileSystemObject")
   set objFolder = objFS.GetFolder(GIFpath)

   'Loop through each file in the GIFpath folder
   for each gif in objFolder.Files
        'Delete GIF files older than 10 minutes
```

```
            if instr(gif.Name, ".gif") > 0 and _
                DateDiff("n", gif.DateLastModified, now) > 10 then
                objFS.DeleteFile GIFpath & "\" & gif.Name, True
            end if
        next
        set objFolder = nothing
        set objFS = nothing
    End Sub

    Call CleanUpGIF("e:\Inetpub\wwwroot\hworkspc")
    %>
```

Create Chart using XML Data

This section illustrates how you can use the Microsoft Office Chart Component to plot data from an XML data stream. The Chart used in this sample is bound to a RecordsetDef in a Data Source Component. The RecordsetDef itself is created from Active Server Pages (ASP) script that uses the XML Rowset definition to return an XML data stream.

First, create a file called GenerateData.asp in your IIS home directory and add the following code to it:

```
<%@ Language=VBScript %>

<%

' GenerateData.ASP
' Purpose: Generates data for the chart

Option Explicit

Response.Buffer = True

' Write out the XML-Data header information
%>
```

```
<xml xmlns:s='uuid:BDC6E3F0-6DA3-11d1-A2A3-00AA00C14882'
xmlns:dt='uuid:C2F41010-65B3-11d1-A29F-00AA00C14882'
xmlns:rs='urn:schemas-microsoft-com:rowset'
xmlns:z='#RowsetSchema'>

<%
    ' Write out the schema info
%>

<s:Schema id='RowsetSchema'>
    <s:ElementType name='row' content='eltOnly'>
            <s:attribute type='XValues'/>
            <s:attribute type='YValues'/>
            <s:extends type='rs:rowbase'/>
    </s:ElementType>
    <s:AttributeType name='XValues' rs:number='1' rs:nullable="true">
            <s:datatype dt:type='string' dt:maxLength='10'/>
    </s:AttributeType>
    <s:AttributeType name='YValues' rs:number='2'>
    <s:datatype dt:type='i2' dt:maxLength='2' rs:precision='5'
    rs:fixedlength='true' rs:maybenull='false'/>
    </s:AttributeType>
</s:Schema>

<%

    ' Now write out some random data
    Dim nXVal           'Temp X value
    Dim anYValues       'Array of values for Y Axis
    Dim nct, nUpperbound, nLowerbound

    nUpperbound = 100
    nLowerbound = 25
    Randomize

    Response.Write "<rs:data>"
    For nct = 0 To 100
```

```
        ' Start the row
        Response.Write "<z:row XValues=' CPU"

        ' Generate and write the X value
        Response.Write CInt(nct) & "'"

        ' Generate and wwrite the Y value
Response.Write " YValues='" & CInt((nUpperbound—nLowerbound
+ 1) * Rnd + nLowerbound) & "'"

        ' Close the row tag
        Response.Write "/>"

    Next 'ct

    ' Close the data section
    Response.Write "</rs:data>" & vbcrlf

    ' Close the xml tag
                Response.Write "</xml>"
%>
```

Then we can create another file named Chart.htm in the same directory as GenerateData.asp to display the chart from XML data. Add the following to Chart.htm:

```
<HTML>
<HEAD>
<TITLE>Sample Chart</TITLE>
</HEAD>

<BODY>
<H1>Chart based on XML Data</H1>

<!— OWC DSC Control —>
<object classid="clsid:0002E530-0000-0000-C000-000000000046"
id="dscSample">
</object>
```

```
<!- OWC Chart Control ->
<OBJECT  classid=clsid:0002E500-0000-0000-C000-000000000046
height=384
id=csSample style="HEIGHT: 75%; WIDTH: 100%" width=576>
</OBJECT>

<SCRIPT language=vbscript>

Sub Window_onLoad()
    ' Initialize the DSC
    DSCInit dscSample

    ' Draw the chart
    DrawChart csSample, dscSample

End Sub

' Initializes the DSC by setting Connection String and RecordSetDef
Sub DSCInit(dsc)
    ' Add a RecordsetDef with name ChartData to the dsc
    if len(dsc.ConnectionString) = 0 then
         dsc.ConnectionString = "provider=mspersist"
         dsc.RecordsetDefs.AddNew "GenerateData.ASP", _
         dsc.Constants.dscCommandFile, "ChartData"
    else
         Window.status = "DSC ConnectionString is already set!"
    end if
End Sub

' Draws the chart using the RecordSetDef data
Sub DrawChart(cspace, dsc)
    Dim c           'Constants object
    Dim cht         'Temp WCChart object
    Dim ser         'Temp WCSeries object
    Dim ax          'Temp WCAxis object

    Set c = cspace.Constants
```

```
' Clear the Chartspace
cspace.Clear

' Load the chart data sources
Dim cds            'Temp WCChartDataSource object
' Add a DataSource to the Chart and set it to be the dsc
Set cds = cspace.ChartDataSources.Add()
Set cds.DataSource = dsc

' Set the Data Member to be the RecordsetDef
cds.DataMember = "ChartData"
cds.CacheSize = 400

' Draw the Chart
set cht = cspace.Charts.Add()
cht.Type = c.chChartTypeLineMarkers
cht.HasLegend = True
cht.Legend.Position = c.chLegendPositionTop
cht.HasTitle = True
cht.Title.Caption = "CPU Utilizations"

' Add a series
set ser = cht.SeriesCollection.Add()
ser.Name = "Utilization(%)"
ser.Caption = ser.Name
ser.Marker.Size = 4

' Set the Categories to the first field (YValues)in the
' RecordSetDef of the DataSource—dsc
ser.SetData c.chDimCategories, 0, 0

' Set the Values to the second field (XValues)in the
' RecordSetDef of the DataSource—dsc
ser.SetData c.chDimValues, 0, 1
```

```
' Set the tick label spacing depending on the number of points
plotted
Set ax = cht.Axes(c.chAxisPositionBottom)
ax.TickLabelSpacing = cht.SeriesCollection(0).Points.Count / 10
End Sub

</SCRIPT>
</BODY>
</HTML>
```

This will create a chart on the web page to display the CPU Utilization Rate from XML data.

Summary

In this chapter, we have covered some advanced techniques for charting on the top of the basic charting techniques that covered on the previous chapter. Some chart types will tremendously benefit from these techniques. For example, data labels will make pie charts much more informative to the users. Split axis can be a handy enhancement when the data concentrated in certain areas. You should also consider whether to create a chart as an object depending on your situation.

In addition we covered how to create unique chart each time and clean up techniques. Since we only covered create charts from database on the previous chapter, we also include a sample for using XML data to create charts in this chapter.

Chapter 5

Introduction to PivotTable Component

The PivotTable component provides interactive data analysis for both tabular and OLAP data sources. Users can simply select the criteria then the PivotTable component will calculate the data and generate reports dynamically.

Another key feature for PivotTable component to generate aggregated values. The PivotTable component can generate summary values for an intersection of categories. In a tabular data source, the PivotTable component can also show the aggregate values for detail data rows. If this option is not being used, the PivotTable component will just display the list of original table rows.

Data Sources

The PivotTable component can work with three different types of data sources: tabular data sources, multidimensional (OLAP) data sources, and XML data sources. In addition, the PivotTable component can retrieve data from Data Source component. We will cover Data Source component in later chapter.

When we talk about tabular data sources, we will naturally think about OLE DB data sources such as Access or SQL Server. Yes, they are tabular data sources PivotTable component can work with. In addition, PivotTable component can also work with non-relational data sources as long as they have some form of textual command syntax or named tables.

Multidimensional (OLAP) data sources composed of *cubes* instead of tables as in relational databases. Each cube has added another dimension of data into a table. For example, instead of having book title and sales volumes of each month in the table format, the cube also shows the sales volumes for each region at each month. Therefore, region dimension has added to the table.

The PivotTable component also works with XML data sources. The PivotTable component supplies the URL to the persistence provider. Then persistence provider uses the Internet services of Windows to request the results of that URL. The results are parsed and loaded into the WCE, and the PivotTable control continues on–Just as it is working with tabular data sources.

The complicated part for the PivotTable component is it uses different connection syntax for different data sources. Table 5.1 shows the property and description of data binding.

Table 5.1: Binding to data

Property	Description
PivotTable.ConnectionString	Set this to a valid connection string to hook up the Pivot Table control to the data source.
PivotTable.CommandText	Set this to a SQL statement or whatever command text the provider will accept. CommandText is used only for tabular data sources.
PivotTable.DataMember	Set this to the name of the OLAP cube you want to use or the name of the data set in the DSC refereed to by the DataSource property.
PivotTable.DataSource	Set this to an instance of the DSC to use it as the data source. DataSource also will return the DSC even when you use the built-in ConnectionString property.

For tabular data sources, you should use the following syntax:

```
Sub ConnectToTable(strTableName, strConn, strSQL)
    strTableName.ConnectionString = strConn
    strTableName.CommandText = strSQL
End Sub
```

For multidimensional data sources, you should use the following syntax:

```
Sub ConnectToTable(strTableName, strConn, strCube)
    strTableName.ConnectionString = strConn
    strTableName.Datamember = strCube
End Sub
```

For XML data, you should provide URL in the syntax:

```
Sub ConnectToTable(strTableName, strURL)
    strTableName.ConnectionString = "provider=mspersist"
    strTableName.CommandText = strURL
End Sub
```

Tabular Data Source Sample

To illustrate how to construct a Pivot Table on the web page, we will introduce this Time Off example. There are three people in the department: Robert Becks, Jr., Charlene Saunders, and Elizabeth Jordon. The tabular view shows all three people's time off records in May and June.

Table 5.2: Sample Time Off View

Name	Days	Month	Type
Robert Becks Jr.	2	May	Sick Day
Charlene Saunders	1	May	Sick Day
Charlene Saunders	1	May	Floating Holiday
Charlene Saunders	4	May	Vacation Day
Elizabeth Jordon	1	May	Personal Day
Elizabeth Jordon	1	June	Floating Holiday
Robert Becks Jr.	1	June	Vacation Day
Charlene Saunders	1	June	Personal Day

The following code sample will show the Time Off view:

```
<HTML>
<BODY>

<p>
<blockquote><blockquote><blockquote><blockquote>
<font size="3" face="arial"><b>Time Off Tracking</font>
```

```
</blockquote></blockquote></blockquote></blockquote>
</p>

<P>
<OBJECT  CLASSID=clsid:0002E520-0000-0000-C000-000000000046
id="Pivot" VIEWASTEXT></OBJECT>

<SCRIPT Language = 'VBScript'>
Function Window_OnLoad()    'Build the Pivot Table

    Pivot.AllowDetails = False
    Pivot.AllowPropertyToolbox = False
    Pivot.DisplayToolbar = False

    'Connect to the database and provide the commandtext for
    the rowset.

    Pivot.ConnectionString = "Provider=SQLOLEDB; " & _
                             "Data Source=[your server]; " & _
                             "Initial Catalog=[your database]; " & _
                             "User Id=[your user id]; " & _
                             "Password=[your password]"

    Pivot.CommandText = "SELECT * FROM TimeOff"

    Dim oView
    Set oView = Pivot.ActiveView

    'Add fields to the row axis and column axis for grouping.
    oView.RowAxis.InsertFieldSet oView.Fieldsets("Name")
    oView.RowAxis.InsertFieldSet oView.Fieldsets("Type")
    oView.ColumnAxis.InsertFieldSet oView.Fieldsets("Month")

    'Add a total for the number of days fieldset.
    oView.DataAxis.InsertTotal oView.AddTotal("Total", _
    oView.Fieldsets("Days").Fields(0), Pivot.Constants.plFunctionSum)
    oView.Totals("Total").NumberFormat = "#,##0"
```

```
'Collapse rows and columns.
oView.Fieldsets("Month").Fields(0).Expanded = False
oView.Fieldsets("Type").Fields(0).Expanded = False

'Hide the Filter axis.
oView.FilterAxis.Label.Visible = False

End Function
</SCRIPT>
</BODY>

</HTML>
```

When you run this code, depending on the speed of your computer and the size of database, you may see the following displays in sequence: "connecting to data source", then "calculating pivot table", and finally the full display of the pivot table:

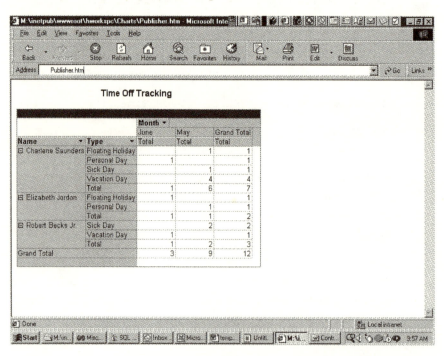

You can click on any down arrow to get a full display of that category's items. For example, click on the name will give you all names:

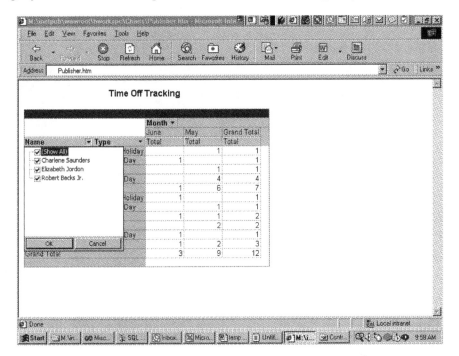

Click on Type will give you all types of time offs such as floating holiday, vacation day, sick day, etc.:

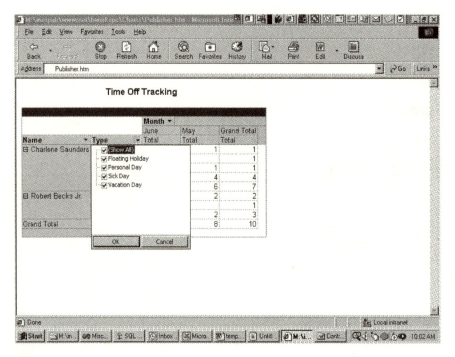

Click on month will show you all the months you have: May and
June:

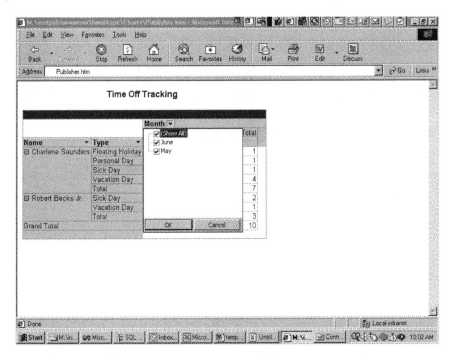

Please note that in every category **Select All** is selected by default to show all records. So you can select the items you want to display, in this example, we deselect Elizabeth Jordon and leave all others to display:

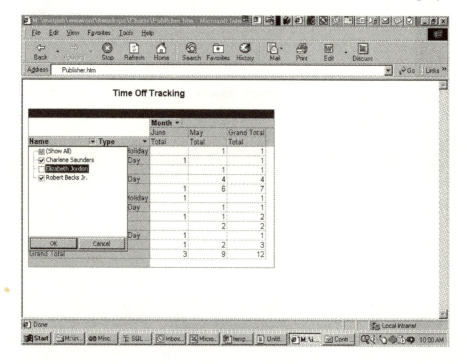

Click on OK, we will get the following results:

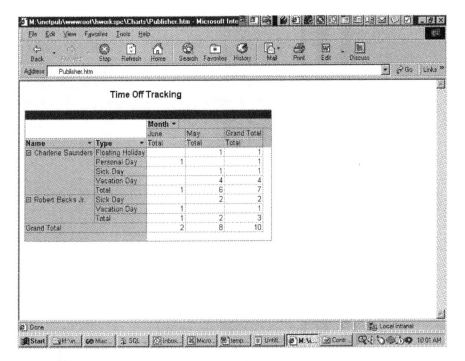

Please note the grand total has been recalculated dynamically.

You can do the same selection for type and month, or any combination of these three.

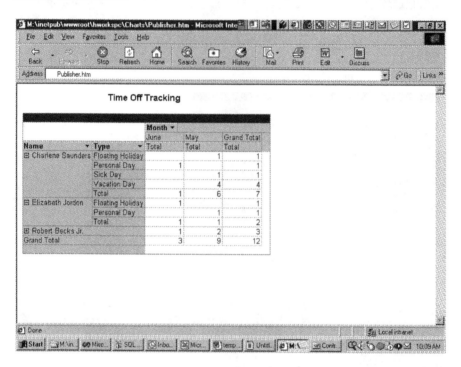

Another useful interaction is the tree view in front of each category. On default, the tree view is expanded into its full display and has a "-" sign in the little square. You can display only the summary of that category by clicking on the square. The "-" sign will change into "+" sign. In the mean time, the display dynamically changed into summary view for that category. We can experiment this action with Robert Becks, Jr. Once we click on the "-" in front of Robert Becks, Jr. the web page will display as above.

When using a tabular data source, every result field is independent in the PivotTable control and is therefore a fieldset with just one field. The exceptions to this rule are data fields and date/time fields. When the PivotTable control encounters a date field in the resultset, it automatically generates two additional fieldsets that provide a calendar-based time hierarchy for the field. One fieldset contains the fields Year, Quarter, Month, and Day while the other contains the fields year, week, and Day.

A fieldset in the PivotTable control contains a set of members, one for each distinct category in each of its fields. Members are display as row or column headings in a cross tab report and are frozen to scrolling so that they are always visible. When using a tabular data source, the PivotTable component creates a member for each distinct value in each result field. It also creates a member called "blank" if it finds any null or blank values in a given field.

The PivotTable control has a few areas that you can use to construct your report. Areas often are called axes in the programming model. OLAP databases also use the term "axis" to describe part of a query result. The row is the region to the left of the control where the row headings are displayed and on which you drop a field to group your data by rows. The column is the region across the top of the control where the column headings are displayed. You can drop a field to group your data by columns. You can place as many fields in these two areas as you want, limited of course by your available system resources.

The filter area is the strip across the top of the control. This area is where you place fields that you want to filter by, choosing one value at a time. For example, you might want to see sales information of one product line, one country, one selected member. You can place as many fields in the filter area as you wan, and if you want the totals for all members in the field, select the "(All)" member. When using a tabular data source, the selection you make in a filter field is used as a local filter on the client. This means the PivotTable control still has all the detail data on the client and is imply filtering the data locally. If you want to filer the data at the server, you must use a WHERE clause in the command text used to populate the PivotTable report.

The data area is the region in the center of the report where the PivotTable control displays totals. Totals placed in this area will cause the PivotTable control to display numbers for the intersections for row and column members. You can add as many totals to the report as you want. The numerical values are displayed in separate columns by default.

The data area is also capable of showing detail rows that are available for a given total.

Tabular Data Source:

Access:

```
Pivot.ConnectionString = "Provider =
Microsoft.Jet.OLEDB.4.0;" & _
"Data Source = c:\program files\microsoft
office\office\samples\northwind.mdb"
```

SQL Server–integrated security (NT and SQL Server)

```
Pivot.ConnectionString = "Provider=SQLOLEDB; " & _
"Data Source=ServerName; " & _
"Initial Catalog=DatabaseName; " & _
"Integrated Security=SSPI"
```

SQL Server–standard security (SQL Server Only)

```
Pivot.ConnectionString = "Provider=SQLOLEDB; " & _
"Data Source=ServerName; " & _
"Initial Catalog=DatabaseName; " & _
"User Id=UserId; " & _
"Password=Passord"
```

You need to change all *italic* names into your specific settings for your database.

PivotTable Component Properties and Methods

From the code sample above, you may need to know more about each property and method in order to construct and customize your table. The following properties and methods are used to adjusting and save the view layout:

Table 5.3: Adjusting and saving the view layout

Property or Method	Description
PivotView.Fieldsets	This property contains all available fieldsets that you can use in the report.
PivotView.Totals	This property contains all available total that youi can use in the repor.
InserttFieldset	Use this method on the row, column, or filter axis to insert a fieldset on the axis.
PivotDataAxis.Insert	Totla Use this method on the data axis to insert a total into the report.
PivotFiled.IsIncluded	Set this property to False to leave a field of a fieldset out of the report. Use IsIncluded to determine whether the filed is in the report.
Expanded	Set this property to True to expand a filed or member and show its children. Retrieve the value of Expanded to determine whether a field or member 9is currently expanded.
PivotView.AutoLayout	Use this method to clear the view for an OLAP data source or to put all fields in the detail area for a tabular source.
PivotView.AddTotal	Use this method to create a new total from a detail field.

PivotField.SortDirection	Use this property to set which way a field should be sorted or to get the field's current sort order.
PivotField.SortOn	Use this property to make the field's members sort by their total values instead of by their captions.
PivotField.SortOnScope	Use this property to sort a set of members based on a total, but only for a certain scope of members on the other axis.
PivotFieldset.FilterMember	Use this property to get or set the currently selected member of a fieldset on the filter axis.
PivotField.FilterMembers	Use this property to get the current set of filtered members for a given field.
PivotField.FilterFunction	Use this property to set or determine the fileter function being used with the FilterMembers property. The filter function can include or exclude members, or ther might be no filtering.
PivotTable.XMLData	Use this property to retrieve the definition of the current report as alarge string that you can save and later reset.
PivotView.TotalOrientation	Use this property to make the PivotTable control display the total captions as row headings instead of column headings.
PivotGroupAxis.Display EmptyMEmbers	Use this property to force the PivotTable control to display rows or columns that are completely emply.

Table 5.4 shows the properties to customize and format the view. Table 5.5 shows some noteworthy events that can be generated by user interaction with the Pivot Table.

Table 5.4: Customizing and Formatting the View

Property	Description
PivotTable.AutoFit	Use this property to turn off the AutoFit behavior, especially for a form-based environment such as Visual Basic.
PivotView.TitleBar	Use this property to adjust the title bar's caption and formatting.
PivotTable.DisplayToolbar, PivotTable.DisplayFieldList, PivotTable.Display PropertyToolbox	Use these properties to control visibility of elements such as the toolbar, field list, and Property Toolbox.
PivotTotal.NumberFormat	Use this property to format the numbers of a total.
PivotTable.SubtotalBackColor	Use this property to make the background color of a subtotal different than that of the numbers that contributed to the subtotal. Subtotalbackcolor is useful for making a visual distinction among different levels of totals in a large report.
PivotTable.SubtotalFont	Use this property to differentiate the font used for subtotals from the font used for the numbers that contributed to the subtotals.
PivotTable.Memberexpand	Use this property to make the PivotTable control automatically expand all fields and members when added to the view.

Table 5.5: Noteworthy Events

Event	Description
QueryComplete	Raised after the PivotTable control has executed a query against the data source, which is commonly a reaction to a change in the report's layout. This is a good time to adjust the report title and any other use interface elements that need to be synchronized with the report.
Click	Fired when a user clicks anywhere on the report. Use the selection property to determine where.
DblClick	Same as click, but is fired when the user double-clicks. Useful for triggering a jump to another page to show details behind an aggregate or perhaps to display the Property Toolbox or your own formatting user interface.
SelectionChange	Fired whenever the selection has changed in the report. Mostly useful when you have other elements on your page or form that should change when new values are selected.
PivotTableChange	Firedd for various reasons when using a tabular data source. The Reason parameter tells you what happened, which includes events such as a new total being created or a total being deleted.
ViewChange	Fired often, so be careful about doing too much in the event handler. Andy slight change in the view causes this event to fire; the Reason parameter indicated what happened.

Summary

In this chapter we covered the basic data sources that PivotTable component supports: tabular, multidimensional, and XML. The PivotTable component can also work with Data Source component to retrieve data. We also offered a complete sample code for Time Off tracking mini application. Finally, we covered some properties and methods of the PivotTable component. In the next chapter we will cover some advanced techniques about PivotTable component.

Chapter 6

Advanced Techniques for PivotTable Component

This chapter will cover some advanced PivotTable Component techniques. We will look at the AutoFit property to constraint the maximum width and height a Pivot Table can resize. We can also decide whether the Pivot Table will collapse or expand its records automatically by setting the auto-expansion properties. Sometimes user may need the table in an image format so they can copy or save the image. The ExportPicture method will allow you to export Pivot Table as an image. We will also cover how to display empty rows and columns. By default, the PivotTable component will not display empty rows and columns. Then we will introduce how to sorting and filtering data.

The second part of the chapter we will cover some advanced techniques to extend and enrich the capabilities of PivotTable component in Office XP OWC environment. The code samples also demonstrate many very useful functionality/behavior implementations:

➢ **Conditional coloring**–this functionality enables users to analyze and find trends in data quickly and easily.

➤ **Actions and Drillthrough**–these are very powerful SQL Server 2000 features that the Web Components do not natively support, but are well supported with these behaviors.

➤ **Printing**–this behavior shows how you can add more features by creating a DLL which interfaces with other automation objects.

AutoFit

By default, the PivotTable component will automatically grow or shrink when you switch the view. This because the AutoFit property is turned on by default. What AutoFit does is to show all the data in the Pivot Table without display internal scroll bars by resizing the Pivot Table. This default setting is useful in most circumstances since the web browser already has horizontal and vertical scroll bars.

But if your Pivot Table is on fixed width form, you would like to turn off the default AutoFit setting. Therefore, you can ensure the Pivot Table will not extend outside the fixed width form. In order to do this, you can do the followings:

➤ Set the AutoFit property at the control's top-level interface to false.

➤ Set the MaxWidth property to the maximum width the Pivot table can extend. The Pivot Table will automatically resize until it reaches the maximum width.

➤ Set the MaxHeight property to the maximum height the Pivot table can extend. The Pivot Table will automatically resize until it reaches the maximum height.

Auto-expansion

The PivotTable component will leave all the fields and members collapsed when they are added to the view. As we mentioned earlier, user can click on the path to view the expanded details. However, sometimes you may need to configure the Pivot Table so it will expand automatically as soon as the data loaded. To expand automatically, you need to turn on the auto-expansion on:

```
PivotTable1.MemberExpand = plMemberExpandAlways
```

On the other hand you can turn off the auto-expansion completely by setting the auto-expansion off:

```
PivotTable1.MemberExpand = plMemberExpandNever
```

By default, the auto-expansion is:

```
PivotTable1.MemberExpand = plMemberExpandAutomatic
```

The value of auto-expansion is taken from PivotTableMember ExpandEnum enumeration.

Export Pivot Table as an Image

In some occasions, we may need to export the Pivot Table into an image file so user can copy and save the table into their local drives or files just like the chart images we discussed on previous chapters. In order to export a Pivot Table as an image, you need to use the ExportPicture method. Here is a code sample for exporting Pivot Table as an image:

```
Set fsoTempPivot = CreateObject("Scripting.FileSystemObject")
strFileName = "PivotTable"
PivotTable.ExportPicture Session("strTempFilePath") & strFileName, _
    "gif", PivotTable.MaxHeight, PivotTable.MaxWidth
Response.Write "<img src='" & Session("strTempFilePath") &
strFileName & "'>"
```

If you would like to have unique name each time, you can modify the strFileName variable to:

```
strFileName = fsoTempPivot.GetTempName
```

You may need to reference the clean up method discussed in the chart component to clean up all the temporary files on the server periodically.

Display Empty Members

If you have any report row or column is completely empty, then the PivotTable component will not display it by default. However, sometimes you may feel the empty columns and rows are significant enough for display. Under this situation, you can overwrite the default setting so the Pivot Table will display the empty columns and rows.

➤ To set the PivotTable component display empty rows, you can use the following code:

```
PivotTable1.ActiveView.RowAxis.DisplayEmptyMembers = True
```

➤ To set the PivotTable component display empty rows, you can use the following code:

```
PivotTable1.ActiveView.ColumnAxis.DisplayEmptyMembers = True
```

Display Total for All Members

As we have showed you on previous chapter, when you change the view, the PivotTable component will automatically adjust and recalculate the total based on the total for all visual members. This is fine for many occasion. Again, in some circumstances you may want to select partial table but still need total for all members. To accomplish this, you have to overwrite PivotTable component's default setting by using the following code:

```
PivotTable.ActiveView.TotalAllMembers = True
```

Sorting and Filtering

Sorting and filtering data in the Pivot Table are key functions that required by many applications. Sorting is to display data in a certain order either ascending or descending order. Filtering is to get a subset of data that meet our criteria from the data we retrieved.

The PivotTable component allows users to perform all the sorting operations through default user interface mechanism, such as toolbar buttons and context menus. You can certainly program the sorting function in your code. The following is code sample:

```
Dim pivotView
Dim con
Dim fs

'Get the active view and the constants object
Set pivotView = PivotTable1.ActiveView
Set con = PivotTable1.Constants

pivotView.Fieldsets(cbxSort1.value).Fields(0).SortDirection = _
        con.plSortDirectionAscending

PivotTable1.ActiveView.DetailSortOrder = Array(cbxSort1.Value)
```

In order to successfully sort you must make sure both SortDirection properties for individual fields and DetailSortOrder array of the active view have been set properly. The SortDirection property of each field you want to sort. The options for SortDirection can be ascending or descending. By default it is ordered naturally.

Sometimes if you get a large set of data, you may need to filter them before creating the table on the web page. For example, we have many types of restaurants in our database but we only need to display Italian, Chinese, French, and American restaurants. The code sample is follows:

```
'Get the active view and the constants object
Set pivotView = PivotTable1.ActiveView
Set con = PivotTable1.Constants

Set fld = pivotView.FieldSets("Promotions").Fields(0)
fld.FilterFunction = con.plFilterFunctionInclude
fld.FilterMembers = Array("Italian", _
                    "Chinese", _
                    "French", _
                    "American")
```

We can also use plFilterFunctionExclude to exclude any type of restaurant we want to exclude. The FilterMembers property will filter the records from the array we include or exclude.

❦ Note–The following techniques are applicable for Office XP PivotTable component only.

❦ Note–You need to install Office Web Component Toolpack in order to view the sample and get the files you need for implementation. Please see the Chapter 10 for install Office Web Component Toolpack for more details.

Behaviors

The Office XP Web Components in general–can be richly extended from the Office 2000 version. This is especially obvious when they are hosted within the Microsoft Internet Explorer environment where the powerful tools that the Internet Explorer platform provides are utilized.

The samples are well commented, providing insight into techniques for implementing your own reusable Web Component behaviors. The PivotTable List samples all use DHTML behaviors to implement their functionality.

Behaviors are "attached" to the object tag which hosts the PivotTable Component, and become in effect an extension of the PivotTable list. Behaviors offer several advantages in the Internet Explorer environment:

➢ encapsulation of specific functionality from other code that may be in the page.

➢ full flexibility to programmatically attach additional behaviors to any DOM object.

➢ the intelligent management of code download and caching.

Each PivotTable list behavior exposes an object model for customizing the functionality of that new feature.

DHTML Behavior Usage

DHTML behaviors can be used via two different methods:

First, DHTML behaviors can be declared at the top of an HTML document as a CSS stylesheet. A CSS property, called behavior, lets a developer specify a URL to a file which contains the behavior functionality as shown in the following code sample:

```
<STYLE>
.MyStyleSheet1
    {
    behavior: url("actions.htc");
    }
</STYLE>
```

This stylesheet can be applied to any DHTML object by using the class attribute. The PivotTable list sample behaviors will only function when they are attached to an OBJECT tag that references the Office XP PivotTable list object, however.

The following is an example of a PivotTable list HTML tag which has the stylesheet attached to it:

```
<OBJECT ID="pt"
    CLASSID="CLSID:0002E552-0000-0000-C000-000000000046"
    class='MyStyleSheet1'>
```

Another method exists for declaring behaviors on an HTML tag. You can declare CSS properties inline on a tag, rather then having to declare a stylesheet at the top of the document. To do this, simply use the style attribute in your HTML tag, and place in quotes the behavior declaration, such as:

```
<OBJECT ID="pt"
    CLASSID="CLSID:0002E552-0000-0000-C000-000000000046"
    style="behavior: url('actions.htc')">
```

By simply adding a behavior to an existing HTML tag, DHTML behaviors make it quick and easy to add useful sets of functionality on top of existing HTML elements.

For individual examples of how individual PivotTable list behaviors are attached to the PivotTable object tag, please see the samples source code. Links to the source code for each of these files is contained within the Office XP Web Component Toolpack Welcome Page.

DHTML Behaviors via Script

DHTML behaviors can also be dynamically added to the PivotTable lists via script using the addBehavior method. This gives a script writer the flexibility to dynamically decide when or if behaviors should be attached, as well as attach behaviors to newly created DHTML objects.

The **addBehavior** method takes one parameter, which is a URL to the location of your behavior as shown in the following code snippet:

```
document.all.pt.addBehavior("drillthrough.htc");
```

Note, however, that adding behaviors via script is an asynchronous call. When addBehavior is called, IE will download the HTC from the server in the background and at some point the behavior will be on line. A developer cannot depend on this happening instantaneously. Thus, a set of calls like the following will fail:

```
document.all.pt.addBehavior("drillthrough.htc");
document.all.pt.Drillthrough.SetAggregate(…);
```

For them to work with dynamically added behaviors, developers will need to hook the onreadystatechange event and place any drillthrough specific code in that handler. Since dealing with asynchronicity is not a simple matter, most developers would probably prefer to use the <STYLE> or "style=" methods of adding behaviors.

Redistributables

Two of the code samples–the Printing Sample and the Cell Coloring Sample–use helper DLL files in order to implement their functionality. The DHTML behaviors do the work of instantiating these DLLs in a page and ensuring that they work.

However, for users who do not have the DLLs installed locally, the DLLs can be installed by using a CAB installation mechanism. What this means is that when Internet Explorer checks and finds that the code is not installed on a machine, it will go ahead and install the DLLs and get them running seamlessly.

A codesigned, redistributable CAB (otphelp.cab) is included with the Toolpack. It is located in the toolpack's common directory (C:\Program Files\Office Component Toolpack\Common\otphelp.cab). When using the Printing or Coloring behaviors in your solutions and if you wish to enable on demand install of the code, you can simply set a property on the behaviors to specify where to get the CAB.

The print behavior has a top level property called **PrintCodeBase** which takes a URL to the CAB file.

A simple usage of this property is demonstrated in the PivotPrint HTM file with this code snippet:

```
document.all.pt.PrintCodeBase = "../common/otphelp.cab";
```

where the PivotPrint behavior has been attached to the **document.all.pt** object.

Similarly, the coloring behavior has a top level property called **ColorCodeBase** which works in the same manner.

Cell Coloring

With the ability to conditionally color cells based on the value, users can see patterns in their data much more quickly. This is done by supplying a HTML behavior that uses the cell coloring add-in to provide some common coloring.

The PivotTable list has a feature whereby you can show underlying OLAP foreground and background colors within a cell. These colors are defined via Multidimensional Expressions (MDX) and thus can be conditional. To turn this feature on, set PivotTable.ActiveView.DisplayCellColor = true. A sample is included in the PivotTable list Code Sample library that shows how to use this functionality. (To view it, go to **Office XP Web Component Toolpack** and click on the **Code Sample Library**. Then click on the **Cell Coloring with MDX** sample.)

Setting cell color using MDX expressions defined either on the client or on the server allows you to show color depending on values other than what is in the cell. For example, a cell could show a value while its color is dependant on how much it varies from budget.

While coloring cells via MDX expression is very powerful and can do many things that the coloring add-in cannot, there are many cases where the add-in is more flexible. For example, imagine that you want to color cells green if they are within the top 10% of all measures shown on a page. To do this, you would need a max value for all the numbers currently visible. Doing this sort of calculation via MDX computation alone may be impossible, or at the least cause something of a performance problem.

The intention for this coloring add-in is to provide cell coloring that is easier to setup, can be applied to any view and is based on the current view. Choosing between using OLAP or add-in cell coloring will depend on what you intend to use cell coloring for.

In terms of implementation, the cell coloring add-in DLL provides no user interface itself, just the ability to programmatically set coloring, and the HTML behavior provides a sample user interface that makes use of the cell-coloring add-in DLL.

User Interface

The Cell Color behavior will add the following **Color Values** context menu commands for aggregates and totals. When multiple aggregates or totals are selected, the commands will still be enabled but only the first aggregate or total will be used as the point of reference.

The "Within n% of top/bottom" command will add two color map segments for the total. One from 0% to n% going from a red to white background; the other from (100-n)% to 100% going from a white background to green. This command will be checked if the aggregate or total currently selected already has this coloring in place.

The "Above n" and "Below n" are only enabled when the selection is one or more aggregates that have a value, where n is the value of the first selected aggregate. These commands add a single formatting segment that colors the background red from 0% to n or green from n to 100%. This command should be checked when the coloring is already set.

Remove Color will remove any coloring for the total.

Programmability

The functionality for conditionally coloring cells is contained within a formatting DLL (OWCPivotFormat.dll). This DLL makes use of some untested infrastructure in the PivotTable list for allowing more coloring flexibility in Pivot cells. Because this infrastructure is not tested or supported, the code that the format DLL uses is not included in this toolpack.

The behavior included makes use of the object model exposed by **IPivotFormatAddin** to add a specific user interface to the PivotTable list, unlike the other DHTML behaviors.

However, the add-in itself does support a lot of flexibility in coloring cells which can be reused by developers. The object model documentation for the core class in the add-in, **IPivotFormatAddin,** is provided below:

Hierarchy

```
IFormatAddIn as IFormatAddIn
    .PivotTable as OWC10.IPivotControl
    .XMLData as String
    .AddFormatMap(TotalName as String) as PivotFormatMap
    .RemoveFormatMap(Index as Variant) as PivotFormatMap
    .FormatMaps as PivotFormatMaps
        .Count as Integer
        .Item(Index as Variant) as PivotFormatMap
            .TotalName as String
            .Enabled as Boolean
            .AddSegment() as PivotSegment
            .RemoveSegment(Index as Variant) as PivotSegment
            .Segments as PivotSegments
                .Count as Integer
                .Item(Index as Variant) as PivotSegment
                    .Begin as PivotSegmentBoundary
                    .End as PivotSegmentBoundary
                        .Value as Double
                        .ValueType as PivotBoundaryValueTypeEnum
                        .BackColor as Color/Integer
                        .ForeColor as Color/Integer
```

➤ IFormatAddIn.PivotTable Property

Attribute	Value
Data Type	IDispatch (but expects a OWC10.PivotControl)
Access	R/W
Default Value	Nothing

This property can be used to specify the Pivot control that is being colored. Setting this to nothing will disconnect the **FormatMap** from the Pivot but does not destroy any format maps.

➤ IFormatAddIn.XMLData Property

Attribute	Value
Data Type	String
Access	R/W

This property can be used to save or restore the state of the add-in. It returns XML describing the current state of the add-in. If the container is Internet Explorer and allows elements to be found by name, then the XML will include the name of the Pivot control. When this property is set, the add-in will search for a Pivot control by name and if found will set the **PivotTable** property to that Pivot control.

➤ **IFormatAddIn.AddFormatMap Method**

Syntax

```
Function AddFormatMap(TotalName As String) As PivotFormatMap
```

Parameter	Type	In/Out	Optional	Description
TotalName	String	In	No	Name of the **PivotTotal** the added format map will apply to.

The **AddFormatMap** method creates and returns a new **PivotFormatMap** that is added to the **FormatMaps** collection.

➤ IFormatAddIn.RemoveFormatMap Method

Syntax

```
Function RemoveFormatMap(Index As Variant) As PivotFormatMap
```

Parameter	Type	In/Out	Optional	Description
Index	Variant	In	No	Numeric index or total name of the **PivotFormatMap** that is to be removed.

The **RemoveFormatMap** method removes the **FormatMap** specified from the **FormatMaps** collection and returns the removed **FormatMap**. If the Index passed is not valid or does not match a **FormatMap** then an error is returned/thrown.

➤ IFormatAddIn.FormatMaps Property

Attribute	Value
Data Type	PivotFormatMaps collection
Access	Read only

This collection can be indexed by total name or integer index. The collection will support Visual Basic collection iteration (for example, the "for each fmtMap in myAddIn.Formatmaps" syntax).

➢ **PivotFormatMap.TotalName Property**

Attribute	Value
Data Type	String
Access	R/W

➢ **PivotFormatMap.Enabled Property**

Attribute	Value
Data Type	Boolean
Access	R/W

➢ **PivotFormatMap.AddSegment Method**

Syntax

```
Function AddSegment() As PivotSegment
```

The **AddSegment** method creates and returns a new **PivotSegment** that is added to the Segments collection for the **FormatMap**.

➢ PivotFormatMap.RemoveSegment Method

Syntax

```
Function RemoveSegment(Index as Variant) As PivotSegment
```

The **RemoveSegment** method removes and returns a **PivotSegment** from the Segments collection for the **FormatMap**.

➢ **PivotFormatMap.Segments Property**

Attribute	Value
Data Type	PivotSegments collection
Access	Read only

This collection can be indexed by an integer. The collection will support Visual Basic collection iteration (for example, the "for each seg in myFormatMap.Segments" syntax).

➢ **PivotSegment.Begin and End Properties**

Attribute	Value
Data Type	PivotSegmentBoundary
Access	Read only

These properties are the begin and end boundaries for the segment of the **FormatMap**.

➢   PivotSegmentBoundary.Value Property

Attribute	Value
Data Type	Double
Access	Read/Write
Default Value	0

This property is the value of the segment boundary.

➢ **PivotSegmentBoundary.ValueType Property**

Attribute	Value
Data Type	PivotBoundaryValueTypeEnum
Access	Read/Write
Default Value	plBoundaryValuePercent

This property qualifies the Value property as a percentage or absolute value.

➢ **PivotSegmentBoundary.BackColor Property**

Attribute	Value
Data Type	Long integer
Access	Read/Write
Default Value	0xFFFFFF (white)

This property sets the cell background color at this end of the segment.

➤ **PivotSegmentBoundary.ForeColor Property**

Attribute	Value
Data Type	Long integer
Access	Read/Write
Default Value	0x000000 (black)

This property sets the cell text color at this end of the segment.

➤ **PivotBoundaryValueTypeEnum Enumeration**

Enum Member Name	Value	Description
plBoundaryValuePercent	0	The segment boundary value represents a percentage of the range of total values for the scope.
plBoundaryValueAbsolute	1	The segment boundary value represents a value that can be directly compared with the total value.

Drillthrough

The OLAP cubes that make up data warehouses contain aggregations–sums, averages, custom calculations–of multidimensional data. However, at times when you view these aggregations you may want to see the underlying detailed records that contribute to that aggregate. For example, if you find sales in the Northwest district were unusually high on a certain day; you may want to see the individual sale records to see a sampling of what people may have been buying on that day. This feature set is known as "drill through" because you are "drilling through" to the underlying records that contribute to an aggregate.

Microsoft SQL Server 2000 Analysis Services introduced support for drillthrough. However, the Office XP Web Components do not have any native support for performing drillthrough operations. The drillthrough code sample adds that support to Office Web Components in a fairly seamless manner.

User Interface

Drillthrough functionality is exposed in a number of different locations. There are three ways to do a drillthrough:

> Double click on an aggregate (total)

> Select an aggregate (total), and click the **Show Details** button on the Pivot toolbar

> Right click on an aggregate, and select **Show Details**

Note that drillthrough takes over the **Show Details** action that the PivotTable list exposes for relational sources but is normally disabled when connected to OLAP data sources. Although showing details in the relational case looks somewhat different, this sample and the native functionality for showing details in the relational case let users accomplish the same scenario: finding out the individual records that contribute to a total.

With the drillthrough sample, the results of drillthrough actions can be shown in two different manners. By default, drillthrough results are shown in a new window in a PivotTable list. The benefit of this view is that the original, aggregated PivotTable list view is still visible in the original browser window, which lets a user to easily continue with their analysis when they are done with the drillthrough data.

A developer can specify an alternate mechanism for showing drillthrough data. When drillthrough is performed, that data can replace the aggregated data within the currently used PivotTable list. Users can return to their aggregated view by clicking the **Show Details** button a second time (the button will have the appearance of the hide details button when drilled in), or they can right click anywhere on the PivotTable list and select **Return to Aggregated View**. As many users may find pages that spawn additional windows annoying, this display mechanism eliminates that problem.

Limitations on Drillthrough

OLAP data sources, almost by definition, can contain high volumes of data. Thus, in a lot of situations when a user clicks on a total in a PivotTable list, the implication and expectation is that drillthrough should get the records that are used to compose that total. Sometimes, there may be hundreds of thousands of records that contribute to a total. Trying to return all of these records may be not only impossible, but it would also not be something that a user may want.

For this reason, drillthrough has three developer-definable limitations that can be specified. These are provided to prevent users from potentially locking their Microsoft Internet Explorer browser when it tries to return far too many aggregate records.

Maximum Number of Records Returned: At the outset, there should be a hard limit to the total number of possible records returned. By default this is set to 25,000 records.

Maximum Number of Records Returned Per Set: A *drillthrough set* (alternatively, a *tuple*) is essentially an intersection of grouping members and filter members. For example, if an aggregate is at the intersection of **Customer.USA** and **Time.1997.Q1** and the data is filtered to only show **Media.TV** and **Media.Radio**, then there are two sets: the intersection of (USA, Q1, and TV), and the intersection of (USA, Q1, and Radio). As there could potentially be a lot of sets, the limit defaults to 5,000 records per set.

Maximum Number of Sets: Each member you filter in creates a new set, and if you filter members from more than one field, you must do a cross product across fields. As an example, if you filter in **Media.TV** and **Media.Radio** as well as **Education.Bachelors** and **Education.Graduate**, *four* drillthrough sets need to be retrieved: (Bachelors, TV), (Bachelors, Radio), (Graduate, TV), and (Graduate, Radio). Adding more filters could exponentially increase the number of sets that need to be retrieved. Note, however, that if you add something to the filter axis but do not filter out any members, that does not factor in this cross product calculation.

Hence, the potential exists where a user may request drillthrough to be performed on a large number of sets. Since each set has a lot of performance overhead, this might be a slow operation even if the total number of records retrieved is low. Thus, the drillthrough sample also lets users control the maximum number of sets to attempt to retrieve, as another way to prevent a drillthrough request from overwhelming the user's machine.

Programmability

The drillthrough sample supports a full object model for manipulating drillthrough functionality:

Hierarchy

```
PivotTable as OWC10.PivotTable
    .Drillthrough as Drillthrough object
            .Constants as DrillthroughConstants Object
            .MaxDrillthroughSets as Integer
            .MaxDrillthroughRecords as Integer
            .MaxDrillthroughRecordsPerSet as Integer
            .SetAggregate(PivotAggregateIn)
            .GetAggregate() as PivotAggregate
            .UserInterface as DrillthroughUI object
                    .GetUseDoubleClick() as Boolean
```

```
        .GetUseContextMenu() as Boolean
        .GetUseToolbarButton() as Boolean
        .GetViewMode() as Integer
        .SetUseDoubleClick(boolean)
        .SetUseContextMenu(boolean)
        .SetUseToolbarButton(boolean)
        .SetViewMode(integer)
        .ShowMaxRecordWarning  as Boolean
.Data as DrillthroughData
        .GetRecordset() as ADODB.Recordset
        .CoreTuple as Tuple
        .Sets as array of DrillthroughSet objects
            .MDX as String
            .Tuple as Tuple
            .Recordset as ADODB.Recordset
```

Events

These events are added at the PivotTable Component level.

DrillthroughInvoke: This event fires when a user has invoked a drillthrough on an aggregate via a double click, context menu, or toolbar button. A **DrillthroughData** object is created.

NewDrillthroughPivotTable: This event fires when a new **Drillthrough PivotTable** has been has been set. A developer can trap this event and do custom layout on the newly created PivotTable list. The user can also cancel the **autolayout** algorithm from within this event.

event.PivotTable contains a pointer to the PivotTable list. A developer can set `event.Cancel = true` to prevent automatic layout of the PivotTable list.

Drillthrough Objects

Properties

Property Name	Class	Description
Constants	DrillthroughConstants	A list of constants that are useful for drillthrough.
Data	DrillthroughData	An object that contains the results of a drillthrough.
UserInterface	DrillthroughUI	An object for controlling user interface options for drillthrough.
MaxDrillthroughSets	Integer	An integer that specifies the maximum number of sets to perform drillthrough upon. If this number is exceeded, the drillthrough operation is cancelled. Default is 100.
MaxDrillthroughRecords	Integer	An integer that specifies the maximum number of drillthrough records to return. Default is 25,000.
MaxDrillthroughRecordsPerSet	Integer	An integer that specifies the maximum number of drillthrough records, per drillthrough set, to return. Default is 5,000.

Methods

Method Name	Parameters	Description
GetAggregate	PivotAggregate	Returns the current PivotAggregate which the current drillthrough pertains to.
SetAggregate	PivotAggregate	Add a new actionable item to the collection.

DrillthroughConstants Object

Properties

Property Name	Description
plDrillthroughViewModeNone	When the user invokes drillthrough, a **DrillthroughData** object is created but nothing further is done (the developer should trap **OnDrillthroughInvoke** and do their own drillthrough implementation.)
plDrillthroughViewModeSpawn	When a user invokes drillthrough, the results are shown in a new window.
plDrillthroughViewModeOriginal	When a user invokes drillthrough, results are placed in the original PivotTable list.

DrillthroughUI Object

Properties

Property Name	Class	Description
ShowMaxRecordsWarning	Boolean	Toggles whether to show a warning if the maximum number of records is exceeded. Default is true.

Methods

Method Name	Parameters	Returns	Description
GetUseDoubleClick		Boolean	Determines whether a drillthrough should be done if a user double clicks on an aggregate.
GetUseContextMenu		Boolean	Determines if drillthrough options should be added to the context menu.
GetUseToolbarButton		Boolean	Determines if a drillthrough button should be added to the toolbar.
GetViewMode		Integer	Current view mode.
SetUseDoubleClick	Boolean	Void	Toggles whether drillthrough should occur if a user double clicks on an aggregate.
SetUseContextMenu	Boolean	Void	Toggles whether a context menu item **Show Details** should be added to the context menu.
SetUseToolbarButton	Boolean	Void	Toggles whether a toolbar button should be added to the PivotTable list toolbar for drillthrough.
SetViewMode	Integer	Void	An integer which specifies how drillthrough PivotTable lists should be viewed. There are three view choices: plDrillthroughViewModeNone plDrillthroughViewModeSpawn plDrillthroughViewModeOriginal Default is plDrillthroughViewModeSpawn.

DrillthroughData Object

The drillthrough data object contains data that constitutes the current drillthrough operation. It is created when a drillthrough aggregate is set. However, actually getting drillthrough records is not performed until (if) the GetRecordset method is called.

Properties

Property Name	Class	Description
Sets	Array of DrillthroughSet objects	Returns an array of drillthrough set objects. Drillthrough sets represent the combination of multiple filter members.
CoreTuple	Tuple	Returns a tuple object that represents the core tuple.

Methods

Method Name	Parameters	Description
GetRecordset	Returns ADODB.Recordset	The recordset that represents the drillthrough operation in its entirety. Note that this method may take some time, so you may want to consider showing a user interface that lets people know that something is happening.

DrillthroughSet Object

Properties

Property Name	Class	Description
MDX	String	MDX that represents the MDX necessary to get a drillthrough recordset.
Recordset	ADODB.Recordset	A recordset that represents the drillthrough set.
Tuple	Tuple object	A tuple that partially represents this drillthrough set. It does not include members that are part of the core tuple.

Tuple Object

Properties

Property Name	Class	Description
Members	Array of PivotMember objects	A list of PivotMembers that constitute this tuple.

Actions

The Action sample is a relatively simple behavior that implements the OLAP actions feature. It adds relevant OLAP cube actions in the right-click (context) menu of the PivotTable Component.

Using a data warehouse built on top of SQL Server 2000 lets a business analyst view critical data. Often times, the numbers they see via a PivotTable list have business implications—in other words, users want to take actions based on what they see in their charts and PivotTable lists. SQL Server 2000 adds support for annotating items within an OLAP Cube with actions. This makes it easy for users to do common tasks related to the data they are interested in.

More specifically, SQL Server 2000 Analysis Services lets an OLAP cube owner annotate virtually any item within their cube. For more information on how you can define actions within a SQL Server 2000 Analysis Services cube, please consult SQL Server Books Online.

Briefly, actions can be associated with many different objects in a cube.

Cubes

Per cube actions.

Example: for the FoodMart Cube, you may have "E-mail cube owner" as a way to let cube customers communicate with cube creators.

Dimensions

Per dimension actions.

Example: for the Customers dimension in Foodmart: "Go to FoodMart Customer Center Web page" would quickly let a user find out more about a customer.

Levels

Per level actions.

Example: for the City level in the Stores dimension in Foodmart: "View FoodMart Global Store Map" would let people know more about FoodMart stores at a broad level.

Members

Actions for members. These are probably the most commonly used sets of actions.

Example: for Alice Cantrell, FoodMart Customer: "Show Customer Report".

Example: for Store 157, FoodMart Store: "E-mail Manager", or "Show Store Location".

Sets

Example: for this group of customers, "Show Contact Information".

Cells

Example: for a certain total: "View total comments" may let you find out more details about a total, like perhaps when the numbers for the total for some reasons are incomplete.

The Action PivotTable list sample supports all of these actions except for Sets, because the PivotTable list component does not support sets.

There are several types of Analysis Server actions that can be created. All of these actions can be fully parameterized using MDX; in other words, actions give developers the flexibility to call a URL where the customer name is part of the URL query string.

URL Action

A URL action will navigate a user to a web page. The PivotTable List Action Sample will open a new instance of Internet Explorer and navigate to the specified Web page.

HTML Action

Here, an OLAP administrator has the flexibility to define HTML that should be shown when the action is fired. The Action PivotTable list sample, in particular, will open a new instance of Internet Explorer and show the HTML that has been defined for the action.

Data Set Action

When this action is selected, the PivotTable list engine will return a new set (a cell set) of data. The PivotTable list sample will open a new instance of the Web browser with a PivotTable list embedded within it.

Rowset Action

When this action is selected, the PivotTable list engine will return a new set (a record set) of data. The PivotTable list sample will open a new instance of the Web browser with a PivotTable list embedded within it.

Statements Action

Executes an MDX command on the current OLAP session. Essentially the same as programmatically invoking Connection.Execute(<string>), this action will serve to modify the existing PivotTable list view.

Command Line

Fires a DOS-style command line. The PivotTable list does not directly support this action, because it would pose a security concern from a web browser if the command line action did not provide sufficient warnings to the user of what was to happen.

Proprietary

This action essentially is a reserved slot for custom solution developers who want to define their own very custom action types. As a result, the Action PivotTable list sample does not directly support proprietary actions, because there is no definitive (or even common) way to implement this action satisfactorily.

Programmability

Hierarchy

```
PivotTable as OWC10.PivotTable
    .OLAPActions as OLAPActions object
        .UserInterface as ActionUI object
```

Events

These events are added at the PivotTable Component level.

BeforeAction—this event fires when a user has invoked an action. **event.Action** contains a pointer to the action object.

If the developer sets `event.Cancel = true`, the action invocation is cancelled.

Action Object

Properties

Property Name	Class	Description
Name	String	Action Name
Caption	Integer	Action Caption
Type	Integer	Type of action Will return one of the following constants: OLAPAction.Constants.plActionTypeURL OLAPAction.Constants.plActionTypeHTML OLAPAction.Constants.plActionTypeStatement OLAPAction.Constants.plActionTypeDataSet OLAPAction.Constants.plActionTypeRowSet OLAPAction.Constants.plActionTypeCommandline OLAPAction.Constants.plActionTypeProprietary
Content	String	Content of the action – for example, the URL if the action is a URL action.
Description	String	User-friendly description of the action — this is something defined in the OLAP server.
Application	String	Name of the application used to execute an action. This is not used in the UI.
ActionableItem	ActionableItem	The parent actionable item of this action object.
Actions	ActionCollection	A list of the actions that this actionable item supports.

ActionUI object

Methods

Method Name	Parameters	Description
GetExposeProprietaryActions	(returns Boolean)	Returns true if the actions HTC exposes actions for proprietary actions.
GetExposeCommandLineActions	(returns Boolean)	Returns true if the actions HTC exposes actions for command line actions.
SetExposeProprietaryActions	(Boolean in)	If true, the actions HTC will expose a user interface for proprietary actions. The actions HTC will not do anything to implement the actions; the coder must catch the **BeforeAction** event and do their own thing.
SetExposeCommandLineActions	(Boolean in)	If true, the actions HTC will expose a user interface for command line actions. The actions HTC will not do anything to implement the actions; the coder must catch the **BeforeAction** event and do their own thing.

Printing

Printing remains an extremely important feature of software today. For summarizing points, nothing really beats having a solid printout of an interesting report.

The Microsoft Office XP Web Components' PivotTable list control does not support printing natively, however. Rather, it relies on its hosting container (for example, Microsoft Internet Explorer) to print it out correctly. Usually, this does not lead to optimal printing of PivotTables. For example, although Microsoft Internet Explorer 5.5 features greatly improved printing support, it does not support all desired features in the context of printing ActiveX components like the PivotTable Component. Problems like row breaks, not respecting page boundaries and not being able to horizontally paginate mean that data may be cropped and hard to read or unreadable.

Microsoft Excel, on the other hand, has rich support for printing out cell tables. Thus, what this code sample does is get an HTML representation of the current view from the PivotTable list. Then, it automates Excel and "pours in" this HTML view. Excel is automated to show a print preview or perform a printout.This gives PivotTable list users all of the power of Excel printing from within their Web browser.

User Interface

The printing sample will add two buttons to the PivotTable list toolbar:

➤ **Print Button** This will print the current view. The user will see a standard Print dialog for selecting the number of copies to print as well as the Printer to print to, among other properties.

➤ **Print Preview Button** Here, the user first sees a preview of what will be printed. From there, they can click the **Print** button on the toolbar to print the report, if desired.

Also, **Print** and **Print Preview** actions are added to the context menu of the PivotTable list. **Print** and **Print Preview** actions in the context menu provide an accessible way for keyboard users to perform these actions.

Programmability

Hierarchy

.Printing *as ExcelPrinting object*
    .Print()
.PrintPreview()
      .GetUseToolbarButton() *as Boolean*
      .SetUseToolbarButton(boolean)

ExcelPrinting object

Methods

Method Name	Parameters	Description
Print()	none	Invokes the **Print** action.
PrintPreview()	none	Invokes the **PrintPreview** action.
GetUseToolbarButton	PivotAggregate	Returns whether this add-in adds buttons to the PivotToolbar.
SetUseToolbarButton	Boolean	Sets whether the Printing add-in should add icons to the toolbar of PivotTable list.

Summary

This chapter covered some advanced PivotTable Component techniques. The AutoFit property to constraint the maximum width and height a Pivot Table can resize. The auto-expansion properties is used to decide whether the Pivot Table will collapse or expand its records automatically. The ExportPicture method will allow you to export Pivot Table as an image. We also covered the sorting and filtering techniques and how to display empty rows and columns.

The second part of the chapter we covered some advanced techniques to extend and enrich the capabilities of PivotTable component in Office XP OWC environment. The code samples also demonstrated many very useful functionality/behavior implementations in conditional coloring, drillthrough, and printing. The information from second part of chapter is coming from Microsoft Software Developer's Network web site: msdn.microsoft.com. You can get more up-to-date information from this web site.

Chapter 7

Introduction to Spreadsheet Component

Working with the OWC Spreadsheet component is very similar to working with a Microsoft Excel workbook object. The methods and properties you use to manipulate the spreadsheet are similar to those you use when you automate Excel. The Spreadsheet component has recalculation engine that dynamically calculate the data just like in Excel. The Spreadsheet component support almost all functions in Excel. Therefore, the Spreadsheet component should be relatively easy to use.

Office 2000 Spreadsheet component supports only one worksheet. But the Office XP Spreadsheet component allows more than one worksheet—just like in Excel.

This chapter we will introduce Spreadsheet component. We start with how to populating the spreadsheet component. Then we overview the properties and methods that associated with Spreadsheet component. These properties and methods are useful for modify and customize the Spreadsheet component.

Populating the Spreadsheet Component

The Spreadsheet component does not own the data container. It loads data from a data container and save it. You can add data to the Spreadsheet component in one of the following ways:

> ➢ Publish a spreadsheet or range of data from Excel with interactivity (see Figure 7.1).

While you are in the Excel spreadsheet you want to publish, you can create a HTML file with an <object> tag for the Spreadsheet component. So when the data published, it no longer refer to the original spreadsheet. To publish your spreadsheet, open your worksheet and choose **Save As** Web Page command from the **File** menu. You will be prompt the following dialog box as show in Figure 7.1. Select **Add Interactivity** then **Save** the worksheet.

Congratulations. Now you have published a Spreadsheet that available to view and edit from web browser with the Spreadsheet component.

Figure 7.1: Publish a spreadsheet with interactivity

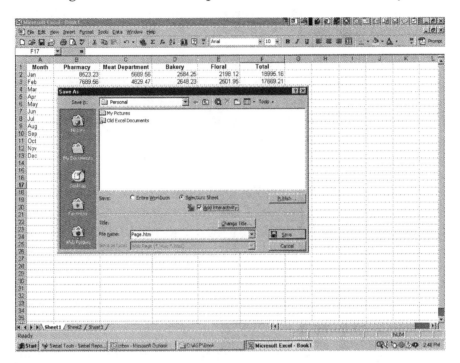

➢ Copy and paste data from an Excel worksheet, text file, or Microsoft Word document into the Spreadsheet component.

✎ **Note**: when you copy and pasting ranges, there are several issues you need to know. First, if a cell in the range has a formula referring to a cell that's not in the range, that on another worksheet, or that in another workbook, Excel will simply copy the current value for that cell but not the formula. So any reference out of copy range will turns into a literal value that equals the value of the reference when it was copies.

Then, not everything from Excel sheet can be copied. For example, a chart in the workbook will be lost during the copy and paste process.

Finally, the protection settings of the spreadsheet will affect not only how the content gets published but also how it gets pasted into the Spreadsheet control. If the source spreadsheet is password protected, the range will still copy and paste, but only retains literal value. If the spreadsheet is protected without a password, then the range will paste normally.

➤ Import data from a text file, Web page, or XML file. These various types of data may be imported by using the Spreadsheet object's CSVURL, HTMLURL, XMLURL, CSVData, HTMLData, and XMLData properties and the LoadText method of the Range object.

➤ Use the Value property of the Range object to assign values to specific cells in the spreadsheet.

The following code will assign values into the spreadsheet using value properties:

```
<HTML>
<BODY>

<OBJECT  classid=clsid:0002E510-0000-0000-C000-000000000046
height="100%"
id=Spreadsheet1 width="100%"></OBJECT>

<SCRIPT Language=VBScript>
```

```
Function Window_OnLoad()
    'Populate the Spreadsheet with data
    With SpreadSheet1
        .Range("A1:B1").Value = Array("Station Number", "Cartons
        Shipped")

        .Range("A2:A13").Value = Array(1,  2,  3,  4,  5,  6,  7,
                                          8,  9,  10,  _11,  12)
        .Range("B2:B13").Value = Array (133890, 135000,
                                        135790, 137300, _
                                        138130, 139100,
                                        139900, 141120, _
                                        141890, 143230,
                                        144000, 145290)
        .Range("A1:B13").AutoFitColumns
        .Range("B2:B13").NumberFormat = "0"
    End With

    With SpreadSheet1.Range("A1:B1")
        .Font.Bold = True
        .Font.Size = 11
        .Interior.Color = "Silver"
    End With

End Function

</SCRIPT>

</BODY>
</HTML>
```

The above code will produce the following spreadsheet on the web page:

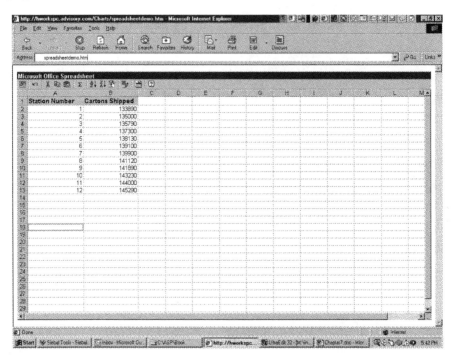

➢ Bind to a data source by using the DataSource and DataMember properties, or by using the ConnectionString and CommandText properties. Since we have covered the similar topic in the PivotTable component, this method should look familiar to you.

The following sample illustrates how you can populate the Spreadsheet component with data and apply various formatting to the cells and the worksheet. You can also populates a worksheet by using the ConnectionString and CommandText. For example, if you want to retrieve data from the Temp database and Temp table, use the following syntax:

```
sCnn = "provider=microsoft.jet.oledb.4.0; data source=" & _
"C:\Program Files\Microsoft Office\Office10\Samples\Temp.mdb"
sSQL = "SELECT * FROM Temp"
oSheet.ConnectionString = sCnn
oSheet.CommandText = sSQL
```

Properties, Methods, and Events

A number of useful properties, methods, and events are useful for the customizing and modifying the spreadsheet. We will look at the summary of these properties, methods, and events then we included an example in Office XP spreadsheet component that uses some of these properties and methods. When you want to use events, make sure the event won't fire constantly and unnecessarily. For example, the Spreadsheet.Change event will fire every time you make a change in the spreadsheet—users may feel annoying.

Getting data into the component

The following properties and methods are used to getting data into the component.

Property or Method	Description
Spreadsheet.DataType	A string based property that tells the Spreadsheet component which of the properties to use for loading data if more than one is set. The value to which you set this property is the name of the other property you want it to use.
Spreadsheet.HTMLData	A string-based property that can be used to get or set the spreadsheet's contents in an HTML table format. The format also contains extra attributes and XML tags that are used to keep information that is necessary to reconstruct the spreadsheet model (such as a cell formula) but that is not part of HTML 3.2 table format. You can set this property to string containing an HTML table, or you can get the value of this property to obtain the entire contents of the spreadsheet when necessary for persistence.
Spreadsheet.HTMLURL	A string-based property that contains a URL from which to load the spreadsheet. The URL must return an HTML document with a table in it. A spreadsheet saved in HTML format from Excel 2000 can be loaded using this property, or this property can refer to an ASP page or a CGI program that builds tables from a database on the fly.

Spreadsheet.CSVData	A string-based property accepts or returns CSV format data.
Spreadsheet.CSVURL	A string-based property accepts or returns CSV format data from URL.
Spreadsheet.LoadText	A method used to load a delimited text file to the spreadsheet. The text file format can use any set of filed delimiters such as comma or tab.

Ranges

The following property and method are used to specify and working with ranges. You can indicate the address of a range, edit cells in the range, format data in a range, and add formula in a range, etc.

Property or Method	Description
Spreadsheet.Range	This method returns a Range object given a range reference (such as B1: E4). You can also pass a single cell reference as a range.
Range.Address	This property returns the address of the range. For example: B3:F8
Range.Cells	This property is used to access specific cells in a range. For example, Range1.Cells(2,4) will return the value of row 2 column 4 in the range.
Range.Columns	This property returns the number of the first column in the range.
Range.Rows	This property returns the number of the first row in the range.
Range.HTMLData	This property is used to get an HTML table representation of the data in a range. The difference between this property and Spreadsheet.HTMLData is this property is read-only.
Range.Value	This property gets or sets a variant value for the range. This property can accept a two-dimensional array of variants for putting data into the range.
Range.Formula	This property is used to read or write the formula string for a cell. You should always include the equal sign (=) in front of a formula just like in Excel.
Range.Text	This property returns the formatted version of the Range.Value property.

Formatting

Similar to Excel spreadsheet, you can format font size, color, range alignment, borders by using formatting properties.

Property	Description
Range.NumberFormat	This property is used to format cell's numeric value. You can either use names to format number such as "Currency" will format numbers into currency format. You can also use number construct to format numbers according to your specific need. For example, you can use "#,###.##" to format numbers such as 2534 into 2,534.00.
Range.Font	A property that returns the common Font object. You can set font name, size, bold, italic, color, and underline properties. For color property, you can also use color code used in HTML.
Range.Halignment	This property controls the horizontal alignment of the range.
Range.Valignment	This property controls the vertical alignment of the range.
Range.Borders	A property is used to set the line weight, line style, and line color of the range border.

Component-Level Appearance and Behavior

You can also modify and customize the spreadsheet in the spreadsheet level. These properties will affect all cells in the spreadsheet level.

Property	Description
Spreadsheet.AllowPropertyToolbox	This property is used to enable or disable the Property Toolbox toolbar icon and context menu.
Spreadsheet.AutoFit	This property is used to control the spreadsheet will or will not automatically adjust itself.
Spreadsheet.Dirty	This property returns true if there is anything has been changed in the spreadsheet.
Spreadsheet.DisplayColHeaders	This property is used to control whether to display the column header. The default of this property is true.
Spreadsheet.DisplayRowHeaders	This property is used to control whether to display the row header. The default of this property is true.
Spreadsheet.DisplayGridlines	This property is used to turn on or off the gridlines. By default, it is on.
Spreadsheet.DisplayPropertyToolbox	This property is used to display Property Toolbox.
Spreadsheet.DisplayTitleBar	This property is used to control whether the title bar is displayed.
Spreadsheet.DisplayToolbar	This property is used to control whether the toolbar is displayed.
Spreadsheet.EnableAutoCalculate	This property is used to control the recalculation engine. If it turns off, the spreadsheet will not recalculate itself. By default, it is on.
Spreadsheet.ScreenUpdating	This property is used to control if the spreadsheet is reflecting the most recent data.
Spreadsheet.Selection	This property will returns the currently selected object.
Spreadsheet.TitleBar	You can use this property to control or format the title bar.
Spreadsheet.ViewableRange	This property will decide which part of the spreadsheet is visible.

Sorting and Filtering

The following properties and methods are used for filtering and sorting cells in the spreadsheet.

Property or Method	Description
Range.Sort	Given a column and sort direction, this method will sorts the selected range.
Worksheet.AutoFilter	This property returns the AutoFilter object that can be sued to set up the details of a current filter.
AutoFilter.Filters	This property returns the Filters collection for the current AutoFilter range. One Filter object applies to each column in the AutoFilter range, and the index of the Filter object matches the column index in the range.
AutoFilter.Apply	You can apply a new AutoFilter by using this method.
Criteria.FilterFunction	This property will control whether the criteria is included in the filter or excluded from the filter.
Criteria.ShowAll	This property controls whether all data will be shown.
Criteria.Add	This method is used to add new criteria to a filter.
Range.AutoFilter	This method is used to turn AutoFilter on for a given range.

Protection

In many cases, you may need to provide some protection to the spreadsheet in order to avoid any accident or damage. The protection properties are used to control the ability to modify the spreadsheet in different ways.

Property	Description
Worksheet.Protection	This property will returns the protection object. With protection object you can set various protection options.
Protection.Enabled	This property is used to control whether the protection in general is enabled.
Protection.AllowInsertingColumns	This property is used to control the ability to insert columns.
Protection.AllowInsertingRows	This property is used to control the ability to insert rows.
Protection.AllowDeletingColumns	This property is used to control the ability to delete columns.
Protection.AllowDeletingRows	This property is used to control the ability to delete rows.
Protection.AllowSizingAllColumns	This property can enable or disable the ability to resize all columns.
Protection.AllowSizingAllRows	This property can enable or disable the ability to resize all rows.
Protection.AllowSorting	This property is used to control sorting of data in the spreadsheet.
Protection.AllowFiltering	You can use this property to control AutoFilter feature.

Undo

The undo properties and methods allow you to undo a number of actions you have performed. For example, you can sort, filter, and change values in a range then undo all of these actions at once.

Property or Method	Description
Spreadsheet.BeginUndo	You can use this method to undo a number of opertions.
Spreadsheet.EndUndo	This method will indicate the end of undo section.
Spreadsheet.EnableUndo	This method will determine whether the undo function is available.

Events

The Spreadsheet component has a number of events available to use. Almost all of the events in the Spreadsheet component pass a single parameter of type SpreasheetEventInfo to the event handler. The SpreasheetEventInfo is a COM object that you can use to retrieve all kinds of information about the state of the application when the event is fired.

Event	Description
Spreadsheet.Change	This event is fired when a change is made to any cell or any range of cells.
StartEdit	This event is fired when a cell is about to be edited.
EndEdit	This event is fired when a cell has been edited.
CancelEdit	This event is fired when a cell edit has been canceled.
BeforeCommand	This event is raised just before a command is processed.
Command	This event is raised just after a command is processed. Actions such as sorting; filtering; inserting or deleting are all considered as command.

Office XP Code Sample

The following example is in Office XP Spreadsheet component that has many of the properties and methods we have discussed earlier. You can following this code sample to create your own customized spreadsheet.

```
<html>
<body>
<button id="btnDemo">Office XP Spreadsheet Demo</button>
<br/>
<br/>
<object classid="clsid:0002E551-0000-0000-C000-000000000046"
id="xpSS" width=400 height=250>
</object>
</body>

<SCRIPT LANGUAGE="VBScript">

Sub btnDemo_OnClick()
    Dim oSheet
    Dim strConn
    Dim strSQL
    Dim iNumCols
    Dim iNumRows
    Dim oToolbarButton

    Dim c
    Set c = xpSS.Constants

    ' Add a new worksheet

    Set oSheet = xpSS.Worksheets.Add(1)

    ' Delete all other worksheets

    Do While xpSS.Worksheets.Count > 1
        xpSS.Worksheets(2).Delete
    Loop
```

```
' Name the new worksheet

oSheet.Name = "Employees"

' Fill the Employees sheet with data from Northwind sample
database

strConn = "provider=microsoft.jet.oledb.4.0; data source=" & _
        "C:\Temp\Samples\Region.mdb"
strSQL = "SELECT * FROM Sales"
oSheet.ConnectionString = strConn
oSheet.CommandText = strSQL

' Determine the number of rows and columns

iNumCols = oSheet.UsedRange.Columns.Count
iNumRows = oSheet.UsedRange.Rows.Count

' Change field names as desired

oSheet.Cells(1, 2).Value = "Region"
oSheet.Cells(1, 3).Value = "Store Name"
oSheet.Cells(1, 4).Value = "Orders"
oSheet.Cells(1, 5).Value = "Total Sales"

' Format field names properties

With oSheet.Range(oSheet.Cells(1, 1), oSheet.Cells(1, iNumCols))
        .Font.Bold = True
        .Font.Size = 11
        .Interior.Color = "Silver"
        .Borders(c.xlEdgeBottom).Weight = c.xlThick
End With

' Add subtotals for Orders and Total fields

oSheet.Cells(iNumRows + 2, 4).Formula = "=SUBTOTAL
(9,D2:D" & iNumRows & ")"
oSheet.Cells(iNumRows + 2, 5).Formula = "=SUBTOTAL
(9,E2:E" & iNumRows & ")"
```

```
' Format columns properties

oSheet.Cells(1, 1).EntireColumn.HorizontalAlignment =
c.xlHAlignLeft
oSheet.Cells(1, 4).EntireColumn.NumberFormat = "#,##0"
oSheet.Cells(1, 5).EntireColumn.NumberFormat = "Currency"
oSheet.UsedRange.EntireColumn.AutoFit

' Sort by Total Sales Amount(column 5)

With oSheet
.Range(.Cells(1, 1), .Cells(iNumRows, iNumCols)).Sort _
      5, c.xlDescending, c.xlYes
End With

' Hide the title bar
xpSS.DisplayTitleBar = False

' Hide the Microsoft Office logo on the toolbar

xpSS.DisplayOfficeLogo = False

' Display the Toolbar

xpSS.DisplayToolbar = True

' Remove the "Refresh All" and "Help" button from the toolbar

On Error Resume Next
Set  oToolbarButton  =  xpSS.Toolbar.Buttons("owc10061")
'Refresh All button
If Not Err.Number Then
      xpSS.Toolbar.Buttons.Remove oToolbarButton.Index—1
      xpSS.Toolbar.Buttons.Remove oToolbarButton.Index
End If
Err.Clear
Set oToolbarButton = xpSS.Toolbar.Buttons("owc1006") 'Help button
If Not Err.Number Then
      xpSS.Toolbar.Buttons.Remove oToolbarButton.Index—1
      xpSS.Toolbar.Buttons.Remove oToolbarButton.Index
```

```
    End If
    On Error GoTo 0

    ` Apply window settings

    xpSS.Windows(1).ViewableRange = oSheet.UsedRange.Address
    xpSS.Windows(1).DisplayRowHeadings = False
    xpSS.Windows(1).DisplayColumnHeadings = False
    xpSS.Windows(1).DisplayVerticalScrollBar = False
    xpSS.Windows(1).DisplayHorizontalScrollBar = False

    `Autofit the component on the Web page
    `so the spreadsheet will adjust automatically

    xpSS.AutoFit = True
End Sub
</script>
</html>
```

Note: The path to the owcvba10.chm Help file reflects the language ID folder (1033) for U.S. English language support in Office. The language ID folder c:\program files\common files\microsoft shared\web components\10\<langid>differs for each language.

Summary

In this chapter we covered the spreadsheet component, its properties, methods, and events. We also includes code samples for both Office 2000 and Office XP version of Spreadsheet component. The code samples should get you started and the descriptions about properties, methods, and events should give your further information for your code development.

Chapter 8

Advanced Techniques for Spreadsheet Component

This chapter will cover some advanced techniques for programming Spreadsheet component. First, we will look at how to program the Spreadsheet component in Visual Basic environment. Then we will introduce how to program Spreadsheet XML. XMLSS is a format that is common to both Excel 2002 and the Office XP Spreadsheet Component, so files in XMLSS may be shared between the two. You can also create your own XSL Transformations (XSLT) style sheets for XMLSS files to transform the data to another format so that it can be shared with any number of applications. XMLSS can persist many of the features common to both the Spreadsheet component and Microsoft Excel and it can also improve performance. At the very last part of the chapter, we give you some information about bugs in the Spreadsheet component.

Programming Spreadsheet Component in VB

Some programmers may need programming Spreadsheet component in the Visual Basic (VB) environment. You can include Spreadsheet component into your VB solutions and add the spreadsheet as part of your form. Instead of create calculation program by your own, you can simply borrow the calculation engine from Spreadsheet component. This section we will cover how to insert a spreadsheet as a control on a Visual Basic form and populate the spreadsheet with data.

First, start Visual Basic and Create a new Standard EXE project in Visual Basic. Form1 is created by default.

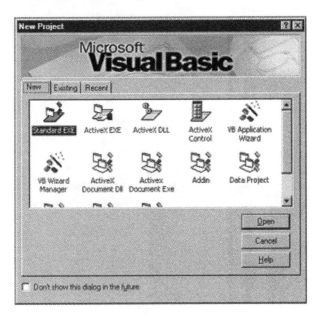

While you are on form1, click on Projects, then select Components. In the Components dialog box, go to Controls tab if you are not in there already. Scroll down the controls list until you find the Microsoft Office Web Component 9.0 item. Select the check box in front of this control and click on OK or Apply. This will Add a reference to Microsoft Office Web Components 9.0 in your Visual Basic program:

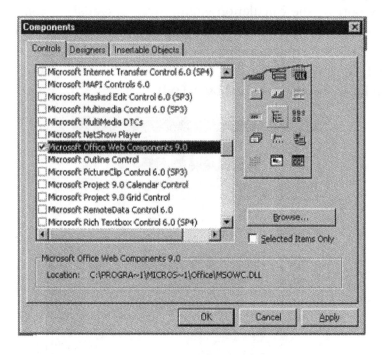

You should be able to see the Spreadsheet component icon has been added to the left side general tools list. Double click on the Excel icon will add the Spreadsheet component onto your form:

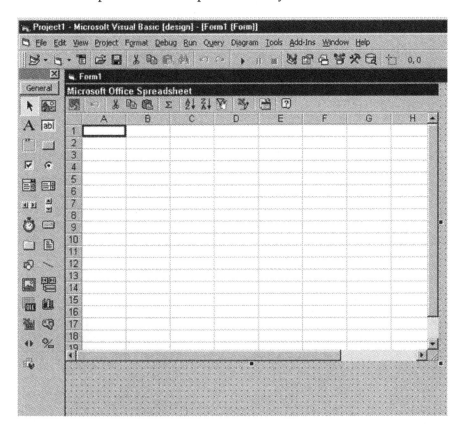

Working with the Spreadsheet control in Visual Basic is almost identical to working with a worksheet in Excel. The methods and properties you use to manipulate the Spreadsheet component are similar to those you would use when automating Excel. The Spreadsheet control can be displayed and used like a worksheet, or it can be hidden and used as a calculation engine for visible controls on the page.

At this point, you can add data to a Spreadsheet control in one of the following ways:

➤ Enter data directly into the grid.

➤ Copy and paste data from an Excel sheet, text file, or Word document.

➤ Import data from a text file or a Web page. For more information see the LoadText Method topic and the HTMLURL Property topic in online Help.

➤ Write code to populate the spreadsheet with data.

🖎 **Note**: that there is no way to bind the Spreadsheet control to data directly.

The following procedure populates and formats a Spreadsheet control with data from the sample database table Vendors in the Access database Operation.mdb.

```
Sub GetNwindData()

    Dim rstVendors As Object
    Dim cnn As String
    Dim strSQL As String
    Dim fldCount As Integer
    Dim intIRow As Integer
    Dim intICol As Integer
    Dim varData As Variant

    'Create recordset and fill with records from Northwind
    sample database.
    Set rstVendors = CreateObject("ADODB.Recordset")
    cnn = "DRIVER={Microsoft Access Driver (*.mdb)};
    DBQ=C:\Temp\Operation.mdb"
    strSQL = "SELECT * FROM Vendors ORDER BY VendorID"
    rstVendors.Open strSQL, cnn, 3 ' adOpenStatic = 3
```

```
'Clear any existing values from the spreadsheet control.
Spreadsheet1.ActiveSheet.Cells(1, 1).Select
Spreadsheet1.ActiveSheet.UsedRange.Clear

'Add the field names as column headers.
For fldCount = 0 To rstVendors.Fields.Count-1
    intIRow = intIRow + 1
    Spreadsheet1.ActiveSheet.Cells(1, intIRow).Value =
rstVendors.Fields(fldCount).Name
Next

'Fill the control with data from the database.
Dim iNumCols As Integer
Dim iNumRows As Integer

iNumCols = rstVendors.Fields.Count
iNumRows = rstVendors.Recordcount
varData = rstVendors.GetRows(iNumRows)

For intIRow = 1 To iNumRows
    For intICol = 1 To iNumCols
        Spreadsheet1.ActiveSheet.Cells(intIRow + 1,
intICol).Value = varData(intICol-1, intIRow-1)
    Next
Next

'Format the headers in row 1 with a Bold Font that is 11 points.
With Spreadsheet1.ActiveSheet.Range(Spreadsheet1.Cells(1, 1),
        Spreadsheet1.ActiveSheet.Cells(1, iNumCols)).Font
    .Bold = True
    .Size = 11
End With

'AutoFit the columns and make all text left-aligned.
With Spreadsheet1.ActiveSheet.Range(Spreadsheet1.Cells(1, 1),
    Spreadsheet1.ActiveSheet.Cells(iNumRows + 1, iNumCols))
    .AutoFitColumns
```

```
        .HAlignment = ssHAlignLeft
    End With

  End Sub
```

This will populate our spreadsheet with data from Vendors table. Now you can working on the data from your VB forms. After you create a reference to the Office Web Components library, you can access Help through the object browser or from the General tab of the Spreadsheet Property Toolbox. You can also locate and double-click the Help file Msowcvba.chm. To get help on a specific keyword, highlight the keyword and press the F1 key. For information about creating references and using object model Help, see Help in Visual Basic or Visual Basic for Applications.

Build Spreadsheet XML

According to Microsoft testing results: Using the Spreadsheet component in server-side code to build spreadsheets provides more scalability and better performance when compared to using server-side Automation of Microsoft Excel.

Automation of Office applications, including Excel, on the server is not recommend by Microsoft and should be avoided when other alternatives for achieving the same results are available to you. XMLSS can persist many of the features common to both the Spreadsheet component and Microsoft Excel; multi-sheet workbooks, cell formatting, Autofilter, cell formulas, and re-calculation represent a handful of those features. The Spreadsheet component has an object model that closely matches the object model for Microsoft Excel. Therefore, if you are familiar with the Excel object model, you can easily apply some of your existing Excel code, with modification, for use with the Spreadsheet component.

The following sample demonstrates how to generate a multi-sheet workbook in XMLSS using the Office XP OWC Spreadsheet component with ASP. The sample also discusses how you can display the resulting XMLSS client-side on a Web page or in Microsoft Excel.

Open your favorite text editor such as Notepad or other ASP editors you use such as Visual InterDev and key in the following code then save the ASP page as SpreadsheetXML.asp:

```
<% Language=VBScript %>
<%
    'Set Response Buffer to true and declare content type as text/xml

    Response.Buffer = True
    Response.ContentType = "text/xml"

    Dim NumOrders, NumProds, r
    NumOrders = 300
    NumProds = 10

    'Declare variables for spreadsheet worksheets

    Dim oSS
    Dim oOrdersSheet
    Dim oTotalsSheet
    Dim oRange
    Dim c

    Set oSS = CreateObject("OWC10.Spreadsheet")
    Set c = oSS.Constants

    'Rename Sheet1 to "Orders", rename Sheet2 to "Totals" and
    remove Sheet3
    Set oOrdersSheet = oSS.Worksheets(1)
    oOrdersSheet.Name = "Orders"
    Set oTotalsSheet = oSS.Worksheets(2)
    oTotalsSheet.Name = "Totals"
    oSS.Worksheets(3).Delete
```

```
'=== Build the First Worksheet (Orders) ===

'Add headings to A1:F1 of the Orders worksheet and apply
formatting
    Set oRange = oOrdersSheet.Range("A1:F1")
    oRange.Value = Array("Invoice Number", "Product ID",
"Units", "Price", "Discount", "Total")
    oRange.Font.Bold = True
    oRange.Interior.Color = "Silver"
    oRange.Borders(c.xlEdgeBottom).Weight = c.xlThick
    oRange.HorizontalAlignment = c.xlHAlignCenter

'Apply formatting to the columns
    oOrdersSheet.Range("A:A").ColumnWidth = 20
    oOrdersSheet.Range("B:E").ColumnWidth = 15
    oOrdersSheet.Range("F:F").ColumnWidth = 20
    oOrdersSheet.Range("A2:E" & NumOrders + 1 _
        ).HorizontalAlignment = c.xlHAlignCenter
    oOrdersSheet.Range("D2:D" & NumOrders + 1).NumberFormat =
"0.00"
    oOrdersSheet.Range("E2:E" & NumOrders + 1).NumberFormat =
"0 % "
    oOrdersSheet.Range("F2:F" & NumOrders + 1).NumberFormat =
"$ 0.00" '"_($* #,##0.00_)"
'Obtain the order information for the first five columns
in the Orders worksheet
    'and populate the worksheet with that data starting at row 2
    Dim aOrderData
    aOrderData = GetOrderInfo
    oOrdersSheet.Range("A2:E" & NumOrders + 1).Value = aOrderData

'Add a formula to calculate the order total for each row
and format the column
    oOrdersSheet.Range("F2:F" & NumOrders + 1).Formula =
"=C2*D2*(1-E2)"
```

```
oOrdersSheet.Range("F2:F" & NumOrders + 1).NumberFormat =
"_(  $* #,##0.00   _)"

'Apply a border to the used rows
oOrdersSheet.UsedRange.Borders(c.xlInsideHorizontal).Weight
= c.xlThin
oOrdersSheet.UsedRange.BorderAround , c.xlThin, 15

'Turn on AutoFilter and display an initial criteria where
'the Product ID (column 2) is equal to 5
oOrdersSheet.UsedRange.AutoFilter
oOrdersSheet.AutoFilter.Filters(2).Criteria.FilterFunction
= c.ssFilterFunctionInclude
oOrdersSheet.AutoFilter.Filters(2).Criteria.Add "5"
oOrdersSheet.AutoFilter.Apply

'Add a Subtotal at the end of the usedrange
oOrdersSheet.Range("F" & NumOrders + 3).Formula = "=SUBTOTAL
(9, F2:F" & NumOrders + 1 & ")"

'Apply window settings for the Orders worksheet
oOrdersSheet.Activate   'Makes the Orders sheet active
oSS.Windows(1).ViewableRange = oOrdersSheet.UsedRange.Address
oSS.Windows(1).DisplayRowHeadings = False
oSS.Windows(1).DisplayColumnHeadings = False
oSS.Windows(1).FreezePanes = True
oSS.Windows(1).DisplayGridlines = False

'=== Build the Second Worksheet (Totals) ===

'Change the Column headings and hide row headings
oTotalsSheet.Activate
oSS.Windows(1).ColumnHeadings(1).Caption = "Product ID"
oSS.Windows(1).ColumnHeadings(2).Caption = "Total"
oSS.Windows(1).DisplayRowHeadings = False

'Add the product IDs to column 1
Dim aProductIDs
```

```
    aProductIDs = GetProductIDs
    oTotalsSheet.Range("A1:A" & NumProds).Value = aProductIDs
    oTotalsSheet.Range("A1:A" & NumProds).HorizontalAlignment
= c.xlHAlignCenter

    'Add a formula to column 2 that computes totals per product
from the Orders Sheet
    oTotalsSheet.Range("B1:B" & NumProds).Formula = _
    "=SUMIF(Orders!B$2:B$" & NumOrders + 1 & ",A1,Orders!F$2:F$"
& NumOrders + 1 & ")"
    oTotalsSheet.Range("B1:B" & NumProds).NumberFormat = "_(
$* #,##0.00    _)"

    'Apply window settings for the Totals worksheet
    oSS.Windows(1).ViewableRange = oTotalsSheet.UsedRange.Address

    '=== Setup for final presentation ===

    oSS.DisplayToolbar = False
    oSS.AutoFit = True
    oOrdersSheet.Activate

    Response.Write oSS.XMLData
    Response.End

'This funtion is used to generate numbers to simplify our
application
'you can also load numbers from database or other sources

Function GetOrderInfo()
    ReDim aOrderInfo(NumOrders,5)
    Dim aPrice, aDisc
    aPrice = Array(10.25, 9.5, 2.34, 6.57, 9.87, 4.55, 6,
13.05, 3.3, 5.5)
```

```
    aDisc = Array(0, 0.1, 0.15, 0.2)
    For r = 0 To NumOrders-1
          'Col 1 is Invoice Number
          aOrderInfo(r, 0) = "'" & String(7-Len(CStr(r+1)),
"0") & r+1
          'Col 2 is Product ID
          aOrderInfo(r, 1) = Int(Rnd() * NumProds) + 1
          'Col 3 is Quantity
          aOrderInfo(r, 2) = Int(Rnd() * 20) + 1
          'Col 4 is Price
          aOrderInfo(r, 3) = aPrice(aOrderInfo(r, 1)-1)
          'Col 5 is Discount
          aOrderInfo(r, 4) = aDisc(Int(Rnd() * 4))
    Next
    GetOrderInfo = aOrderInfo
End Function

'This function is used to compose Product ID

Function GetProductIDs()
    ReDim aPIDs(NumProds, 1)
    For r = 0 To NumProds-1
          aPIDs(r, 0) = r+1
    Next
    GetProductIDs = aPIDs
End Function
%>
```

To display the sample XMLSS on a Web page, you need only set the XMLURL property for a Spreadsheet Component to the URL for the ASP, as follows:

```
<html>
<body>
<object classid="clsid:0002E551-0000-0000-C000-000000000046"
id="Spreadsheet1">
<param name="XMLURL" value="http://YourWebServer/SpreadsheetXML.asp">
</object>
</body>
</html>
```

Once you open the web page, you should be able to see the spreadsheet as usual.

Bugs

Yes, there are bugs in the Spreadsheet component just like many other software on the market. Programmers do not always write bug free code is a fact.

The first bug we want to tell you is date bug.

In the Microsoft Office Spreadsheet Component, the value 0 evaluates to the date December 30, 1899 and the value 1 evaluates to December 31, 1899. This is different from Microsoft Excel. In Excel, the value 0 evaluates to January 0, 1900 and the value 1 evaluates to January 1, 1900. The date January 0, 1900 does not exist in the Microsoft Office Spreadsheet Component.

In addition, the Office Spreadsheet Component does not recognize the year 1900 as a leap year. After March 1, 1900, however, dates in the Microsoft Office Spreadsheet Component and Microsoft Excel begin to match.

The second bug is about the display of Spreadsheet component on the web site. If you attempt to view a Microsoft Excel-based Web Spreadsheet Component in a Web page, the Web page may open as expected, but the Spreadsheet Component may not be displayed correctly. Specifically, the worksheet cells are displayed but the Web Spreadsheet Component toolbar is missing. This behavior can occur if the Mscomctl.ocx file is not registered correctly.

To work around this issue, register the Mscomctl.ocx file. To do this, type the following at the command prompt:

```
regsvr32 mscomctl.ocx
```

Regsvr32.exe is included with Microsoft Internet Explorer 3.0 or later, Microsoft Windows 95 OEM Service Release 2 (OSR2) or later, and Microsoft Windows NT 4.0 Service Pack 5 (SP5) or later. Regsvr32.exe is installed in the System folder (Microsoft Windows Millennium Edition [Me], Windows 98, and Windows 95) or System32 folder (Windows NT). The following syntax and command-line options (switches) can be used with RegSvr32.exe:

```
Regsvr32 [/u] [/n] [/i[:cmdline]] dllname

Switch  Function
   /u   Unregister server
   /i   Call DllInstall passing it an optional [cmdline];
        when used with /u, calls dll uninstall
   /n   Do not call DllRegisterServer; this option must
        be used with /i
```

Summary

In this chapter we covered some advanced topics for the spreadsheet component. In order to make your Visual Basic forms more powerful and utilize the abilities of Spreadsheet component, we first introduced the process of bring Spreadsheet component into VB forms.

Then, we introduced the techniques of creating XMLSS file. XMLSS is a format that is common to both Excel 2002 and the Office XP Spreadsheet Component, so files in XMLSS may be shared between the two.

Finally, we looked at some bugs come with Spreadsheet component. Bugs can be troublesome at sometimes. Especially when you do not have much knowledge about them. We hope this will be helpful to you as a developer to know the symptom and the fixes about the bugs.

Chapter 9

Date Source Component

The Data Source component is best understood as the reporting engine behind data access pages, PivotTable component, and data-bound Chart component. The Data Source component has no visual representation. It is designed to manage the connection to the underlying data source and deliver records to be displayed by other controls on a Web page.

The Data Source component relies on ADO for connections to relational data sources such as Microsoft Access, Microsoft SQL Server, or Oracle databases. Although the Data Source component can provide data to the PivotTable List component, the Data Source component cannot be bound to multidimensional data sources; transformations of relational data to multidimensional data are managed by the PivotTable Service.

✤ **Note**: If you are creating a PivotTable list from a relational data source, the PivotTable Service is used to create a multidimensional data cube from the relational data bound to the Data Source control. Then, this data cube is used by the PivotTable List control. For multidimensional data sources, the PivotTable List control relies upon an OLE DB for online analytical processing (OLAP) provider. The PivotTable Service is the OLE DB for OLAP provider for Microsoft SQL Server OLAP Services.

Introduction

The Data Source component is working behind of each data-bound controls and code to retrieve data, synchronizing user interface, and maintain the notion of current row. The Data Source component is invisible at runtime but it is a crucial part of Office Web components. Without the Data Source component, Spreadsheet component, Chart component, and PivotTable component will unable to connect to database. The Data Source component generates the appropriate commands to produce a hierarchial Recordset at runtime. You can use the Data Source component to do the following:

➢ Associate a DataSourceControl object with a database connection.

➢ Add a record (row) source (table, view, stored procedure, or SQL statement) to a Data Source control.

➢ Provide an ADO recordset to data-consuming objects on a Web page. These objects include the Microsoft Internet Explorer built-in controls that can be data bound, such as the TEXT or SELECT control, and all of the other Office Web Component controls.

➢ Build SQL commands to request data from relational data sources.

➢ Construct hierarchical (shaped) Recordset objects from one or more data providers by using the services of the Microsoft Data Shaping Service for OLE DB service provider.

➢ Persist data in an Office Web Component to a file or load data from a file to an Office Web Component.

Note: Although you can work directly with the Data Source control, in many cases you are not required to. For example, when you create an Access data access page and add fields to the page by dragging them from the field list, Access automatically adds a properly configured Data Source component to the page.

The Data Source component implements the standard COM interface for data source controls, known as IDataSource. This interface is recognized in Microsoft Visual Basic and Internet Explorer environment. The Data Source component automatically participate in those environments' standard data-binding mechanisms.

The following chart shows the Data Source component's data access structure:

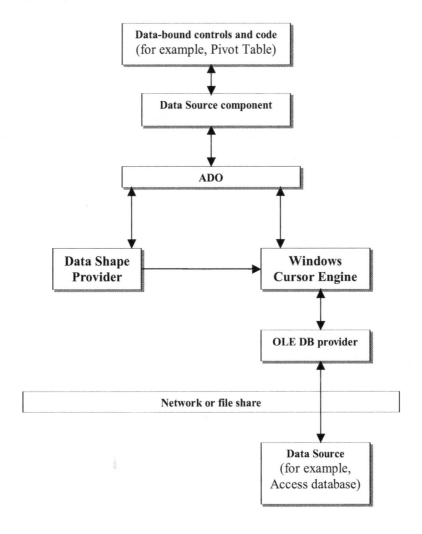

The primary functions of the Data Source component are to connect to data sources, to build and execute commands against those data sources, and to retrieve and bind the results of those commands to elements on the page. Additionally, the Data Source component keeps track of the record the user is currently working with. For more complex "banded" pages, the Data Source creates hierarchical groupings. For instance, you can display an order form with a subform that displays the order details from a related table, or a sales report that groups data by multiple levels, such as nested groupings by month, region, and sales representative.

Data access pages are designed to reproduce many of the features of Microsoft Access forms and reports in Web pages running in Microsoft Internet Explorer 5.0 or later. Beyond simply reproducing forms and reports, data access pages also provide additional features and benefits that are tailored to performing data browsing, data entry, reporting, and analysis from a Web browser.

When you create a new data access page in Access, it inserts an <OBJECT> tag that defines the Data Source component in the HEAD element of the data access page. The ID attribute of the <OBJECT> tag created for a data access page created in Access is always set to MSODSC.

If you open a data access page in the Microsoft Script Editor from Access XP (by opening the data access page in Design View, and then clicking Microsoft Script Editor on the toolbar), you should see the <OBJECT> tag for the Data Source component near the top of the page. Following the CLASSID attribute for the control is an extensive XML definition of properties of the control, such as the ConnectionString property and the ElementExtensions collection. The ElementExtensions collection is used to add custom properties to the data-bound HTML elements in a data access page, and only exists after fields are bound to a page.

Data Source component Objects

Because the Data Source component is designed to integrate with HTML elements, its object model contains members such as the HTMLContainer property of the Section object that allow your script to access the collections, properties, and methods of the DHTML Document Object Model. This, in turn, enables you to work with the HTML elements that make up a data access page.

In addition to interacting with and integrating portions of the DHTML Document Object Model, the Data Source component encapsulates ADO functionality for working with the recordsets exposed through the page. Because these recordsets can be hierarchical and may contain calculated columns that are generated at run time (also known as shaped recordsets), the encapsulated ADO functionality operates in conjunction with the OLE DB MSDataShape Provider and the OLE DB Cursor Engine, in conjunction with the actual data provider for the data source itself.

While the Data Source component is designed to manage most of the details of working with these data access components for you, the Data Source component object model also includes members that allow you to access ADO objects; for example, the Connection property of the DataSourceControl object lets you access the ADO Connection object for the page's data source, and the Recordset property of the DataPage object lets you access the ADO Recordset object for a particular set of records displayed in a page.

While the Data Source component exposes a variety of collections and objects, the primary set of objects you need to understand and work with when customizing a data access page are: the Section object, the GroupLevel object, the DataPage object, and the ElementExtension object.

The Section Object

At design time, a section can be thought of as a two-dimensional container for laying out the controls and elements of your data access page. When you start creating a data access page in Design View, Access adds a single unbound section that has no particular type. A section starts out as unbound, because at the start of the design process the Data Source component for the page doesn't have any Recordset objects defined in its Recordsets collection to bind to. There are two ways to bind data to a section:

- Dragging fields or tables from the Field List into the section

- Setting the RecordSource property in the section's property sheet

Binding the unbound section by either method makes the section a header section and automatically adds a navigation section associated with the new header section. Both binding mechanisms automatically add Recordset objects to the Recordsets collection of the Data Source component associated with the page. The fields defined by the generated Recordset objects become available for binding controls within the section by setting their ControlSource property to the desired field's name.

If you drag fields or tables from the Field List, Access sets the ID attribute for the control to the same name as the bound field (or generates a unique name if there are duplicate names) and sets the ControlSource property for the control to bind it.

If you bind a section by setting the RecordSource property, and then add controls to the section from the Toolbox, you must specify the ControlSource property for the control manually.

❧Note: You can see the organization of the data bound to a page (which is called the data model) by displaying the Data Outline. To display the Data Outline, open a data access page in Design View;

point to Toolbars on the View menu, and then click Data Outline. You can view and set the properties of the items that make up the data model, such as GroupingDef, PageField, PageRowSource, and Recordset objects, by right-clicking an item in the outline, and then clicking Properties.

❧ **Note:** When Access binds a section to data, it sets the ID attribute of the <DIV> tag for the section to reflect the tables that the section is bound to. Don't change the ID attribute for a section in the Microsoft Script Editor, because it can interfere with the data binding for a page. Also, if you add other fields to a section in Design View, Access may change the ID attribute of a section. For this reason, you should complete the basic design for your data access page before adding scripts to the page. Otherwise, you'll need to update any <SCRIPT> tags and code that refers to old ID attributes for the section or the controls in that section.

At run time, the Section object functions as an abstraction for the HTML DIV element and the HTML controls and elements that make up a particular section. The Section object provides methods and properties that allow you to work with a section at runtime.

The Section object provides the NextSibling, PreviousSibling, NextSection, and PreviousSection properties to let you navigate from section to section. To determine which of these properties to use, you need to understand what a sibling is. Sibling sections refer all of the sections at the same grouping level. So if you want to move only between sections at the same grouping level, use the NextSibling and PreviousSibling properties. The NextSection and PreviousSection properties move between sections regardless of their grouping level, but can't access sections that are collapsed, so you can use these properties to move between all of the visible sections on a page.

The NextSibling, PreviousSibling, NextSection, and PreviousSection properties don't distinguish between what type of section they are navigating to. If you need to determine what type of section you have before acting on it, you can use the Type property of the Section object.

In Table 9.1 below, the Type property returns one of the listed SectTypeEnum constants, which have the specified literal value.

Table 9.1: SectTypeEnum constants returned by the Type property

Constant	Value
sectTypeCaption	1
sectTypeFooter	3
sectTypeHeader	2
sectTypeRecNav	4

❧Note: If you want to use named constants that are defined for members of the Data Source component object model from script, you can use the Constants property of the DataSourceControl object. For example, the expression MSODSC.Constants.sectTypeCaption returns the literal value of the sectTypeCaption constant.

If you need a starting point for navigating between sections, you can use the FirstSection property of the DataPage object to return the first section on the specified data page. To test whether a section is expanded, you can use the IsExpanded property of the Section object. To expand or collapse sections, you can use the Expand and Collapse methods of the Section object.

The GroupLevel Object

The GroupLevel object represents the set of sections and records at a given level of the data access page hierarchy. As described previously, each grouping level can have up to four different sections: the caption section, header section, footer section, and record navigation section—plus all sections within a grouping level are referred to as siblings.

The GroupLevel object primarily acts as a bridge between the sections in that grouping level and the set of records to which it is bound. In addition to providing properties that let you define grouping itself, such as the GroupOn and GroupInterval properties that determine the interval used to group items of a given data type, the GroupLevel object also provides properties that control how a user can interact with the data in a group level, such as the AllowAdditions and AllowDeletions properties.

✎ **Note:** Although Access Help lists all of the properties of the GroupLevel object as being read/write, this is only true when you are using Visual Basic for Applications code to work with a data access page that is open in Design View. At run time, all of the GroupLevel object properties except the DefaultSort and ExpandedByDefault properties are read-only. If you try to set any of the other properties of the GroupLevel object, the Data Source component will return, "Run-time error 26072–Property cannot be set in this mode."

Grouping in data access pages is very similar to grouping in reports. However, unlike reports, even simple pages that display a flat set of records with no grouping hierarchy have one grouping level. Architecturally, this allows the GroupLevel object to provide a set of properties that are common to both simple and banded pages. Additionally, your code may need to distinguish between the types of pages; for example, the values for data-bound controls are exposed as single values for simple pages and as an array of values for banded pages.

You can use the Count property of the GroupLevels collection and the DataPageSize property of the GroupLevel object to determine whether you are working with a simple page or banded page. The Count property returns the number of group levels, and the DataPageSize property returns or sets the number of records displayed at time in a particular group level. If the Count property and DataPageSize property are both 1, then you are working with a simple page. If either property returns 1, then you are working with a banded page.

The DataPage Object

While the name of the DataPage object would seem to imply that it represents the data access page itself, this is not the case. A DataPage object represents one of the sets of records that are bound to the sections that comprise a grouping level. The DataSourceControl object maintains the DataPages collection that contains all of the DataPage objects for the page. A DataPage object exists only at run time, and is only created when necessary, such as when one of the repeated bands within a grouping level is expanded. As a result, on a banded page with two or more grouping levels, the number of DataPage objects in DataPages collection will vary depending on how many bands are expanded.

As a general rule, for banded pages you can think of a DataPage object as representing the recordset bound to a set of sections that share a common record navigation control. The topmost node in the grouping hierarchy will have a single DataPage object, and each expanded node within that grouping hierarchy will have its own DataPage object.

A simple page has only one grouping level, and as a result will always have only one DataPage object associated with the single header section of the page.

The DataPage object provides recordset-level operations to the programmer, such as the MoveFirst, MoveLast, MoveNext and MovePrev methods that allow you to move between records in a given grouping level. The Filter and IsFilterOn properties and the ApplyFilter and ToggleFilter methods let you define and apply a client-side filter to a grouping level's records.

The DataPage object also provides a Recordset property that lets you access the ADO Recordset object that is bound to a particular Section object. If you need to perform recordset operations that are beyond those provided for the DataPage object itself, you can use standard ADO code to work with the Recordset object for the section.

The DataPage object also provides a programmatic bridge between GroupLevel objects and Section objects. For example, the name of the recordset definition that is bound to a section is determined by the RecordSource property of the GroupLevel object.

The ElementExtension Object

The Data Source component maintains a collection of ElementExtension objects. An ElementExtension object is used to add custom data-related properties to HTML elements on the page, such as bound text boxes, list boxes, and span controls. The ElementExtension object architecture provided the developers of Access with a way to extend the properties of the HTML intrinsic controls on the page without cluttering the HTML.

ElementExtension objects exist primarily to support the data access page Design View, and for developers who want to create data access pages from Visual Basic code. Most of the properties of the ElementExtension object are read-only when accessed from script in the page at run time. To view the ElementExtension properties, you can set in Design View, right-click a control, click Element Properties, and then click the Data tab.

Although Access Help lists all of the properties of the ElementExtension object as being read/write, this is only true when you are using Visual Basic for Applications code to work with a data access page that is open in Design View. At run time, all of the ElementExtension object properties except for the DefaultValue, Format and TotalType properties are read-only. If you try to set any of the other properties of the ElementExtension object, the Data Source component will return, "Run-time error 26072–Property cannot be set in this mode."

If you set one of the read/write properties of an ElementExtension object at run time, the Data Source component will not automatically repaint the displayed record to reflect this change. To force the record to repaint, retrieve the bookmark for the current record by using the Recordset property of the DataPage object, and set it back to itself. The following code fragment demonstrates how to change the Format property of a control to either "Currency" or "Euro Currency" based on the value selected in a combo box. This code is written as an event procedure for the DHTML onchange event of a combo box named FormatType that has two options: "Euro" or "Currency."

Data Source component events

All Data Source component events take a single argument, which is a DSCEventInfo object. A DSCEventInfo object is a data structure that returns a set of properties that contain information about the event that was triggered. For consistency, the same structure is used for all events, but only the appropriate properties for each event are returned. (See Table 9.3, which summarizes the Data Source component events for a listing of the DSCEventInfo object properties supported by each event.)

Table 2 below lists the properties provided by the DSCEventInfo object. Property names followed by "(new)" were added to object model for the DSCEventInfo object in the Microsoft Office XP Web Components.

Table 9.2: DSCEventInfo object properties

DSCEventInfo property	Description
DataPage	Returns a **DataPage** object for the section that triggered the event.
DisplayAlert (new)	Returns or sets a **DscDisplayAlert** constant that indicates whether or not an alert will be displayed when the **BeforeDelete** and **BeforeOverwrite** events are triggered. This property is read/write. The **DscDisplayAlert** constants are: • **DscDataAlertContinue** – An alert is not displayed. • **DscDataAlertDisplay** – An alert is displayed asking the user to confirm the action.
Error	Returns an ADO **Error** object that contains information about the triggered event.
PercentComplete (new)	Returns a **Long** value that represents the completed portion of the current operation. A value of 100 indicates that the operation is complete. This property is supported only by the **RecordsetSaveProgress** event. This property is read-only.
ReturnValue	Returns or sets a **Boolean** value representing the return value for the specified event. You can cancel the default action for some events by setting this property to **False**. This property is read/write.
Section	Returns a **Section** object that represents the section that triggered the event.

Status (new)	Returns a **DscStatusEnum** constant that represents the status of the current event. This property is supported only by the **AfterDelete** event. This property is read-only. The **DscStatusEnum** constants are: • **dscDeleteCancel** – The delete operation succeeded. • **dscDeleteOK** – The delete operation was canceled through code. • **dscDeleteUserCancel** – The delete operation was canceled by the user.

Table 9.3 below summarizes the events provided by the Data Source control. Event names followed by "(new)" are new events that were added to object model for the Data Source component of the Microsoft Office XP Web Components.

Table 9.3: DSCEventInfo object properties

Event	Description
AfterDelete (new)	Occurs after a record has been deleted, or the deletion of a record has been canceled. Use this event if you want to perform a set of actions when a record is deleted. This event supports the **Status, DataPage**, and **Section** properties of the **DSCEventInfo** object. Note If the deletion has succeeded, the **Section** property will return a value of **Nothing**, because the section has already been removed from the document.
AfterInsert (new)	Occurs after a record has been inserted (added). Use this event if you want to perform a set of actions when a record is inserted. This event supports the **DataPage** and **Section** properties of the **DSCEventInfo** object.

AfterUpdate (new)	Occurs after a record is updated with new data or the record loses focus. This event supports the **DataPage** and **Section** properties of the **DSCEventInfo** object.
BeforeCollapse	Occurs when the collapse control is clicked, or the **Collapse** method of the **DataPage** object is used to collapse a band on a data access page. This event supports the **ReturnValue** and **Section** properties of the **DSCEventInfo** object.
BeforeDelete (new)	Occurs before a record is deleted. Use this event if you want to apply a set of conditions before a record is deleted. This event supports the **ReturnValue, DataAlert, DataPage,** and **Section** properties of the **DSCEventInfo** object.
BeforeExpand	Occurs whenever the expand control is clicked or the **Expand** method of the **DataPage** object is used to expand a band on a data access page. This event supports the **ReturnValue** and **Section** properties of the **DSCEventInfo** object.
BeforeFirstPage	Occurs before the first set of records is displayed on a banded data access page. This event supports the **ReturnValue** and **DataPage** properties of the **DSCEventInfo** object.
BeforeInitialBind (new)	Occurs before the controls on the specified data access page are bound to the recordset for the first time. Use this event to set the properties for the data access page before the controls are populated with data. Note If code written for this event performs an operation that requires the **Data Source component** to fetch data, the controls in the page will be populated when you do so. For example, when using the **Connection** or **DefaultRecordset** properties to retrieve ADO **Connection** and **Recordset** objects for the page, and then using methods that retrieve data against them. This event supports none of the properties of the **DSCEventInfo** object.
BeforeInsert (new)	Occurs when the user clicks the **New** button on the navigation toolbar. This event supports the **ReturnValue, DataPage,** and **Section** properties of the **DSCEventInfo** object.
BeforeLastPage	Occurs before the last set of records is displayed on a banded data access page. This event supports the **ReturnValue** and **DataPage** properties of the **DSCEventInfo** object.
BeforeNextPage	Occurs before the next set of records is displayed on a banded data access page. This event supports the **ReturnValue** and **DataPage** properties of the **DSCEventInfo** object.

BeforeOverwrite (new)	Occurs when an existing XML or schema file is about to be overwritten when using the **ExportXML** method.
	This event supports the **ReturnValue** and **DataAlert** properties of the **DSCEventInfo** object.
	      Important This event doesn't fire when the data access
	      page is running in Internet Explorer. It does fire if the
	      Data Source component is running in a Visual Basic
	      application or an HTML application (HTA).

BeforePreviousPage	Occurs before the previous set of records is displayed on a banded data access page. This event supports the **ReturnValue** and **DataPage** properties of the **DSCEventInfo** object.
BeforeUpdate (new)	Occurs when data is changed, but before the recordset is updated. Use this event to validate data before it is committed to the database. This event supports the **ReturnValue**, **DataPage**, and **Section** properties of the **DSCEventInfo** object.
Current	Occurs when a record becomes the current record. This event supports the **DataPage** and **Section** properties of the **DSCEventInfo** object.
DataError	Occurs whenever a data error occurs. This event supports the **Error** property of the **DSCEventInfo** object.
DataPageComplete	Occurs when the specified data access page finishes loading. This event supports the **DataPage** property of the **DSCEventInfo** object.
Dirty (new)	Occurs when the user changes the contents of a record on a data access page. This event fires before the **BeforeUpdate** event. This event supports the **ReturnValue**, **DataPage**, and **Section** properties of the **DSCEventInfo** object.
Focus (new)	Occurs when a section in a data access page receives focus. This event supports the **DataPage** and **Section** properties of the **DSCEventInfo** object.

RecordExit (new)	Occurs when the user navigates to another record, refreshes the data access page, or closes the data access page. This event occurs after the **BeforeUpdate** event, but before the record is changed. In the case of a banded data access page, moving among child records for the same parent does not fire this event.
	This event supports the **ReturnValue**, **DataPage**, and **Section** properties of the **DSCEventInfo** object.
	Important There is no way to programmatically control whether a user can close the browser or navigate away from the page, which will end the processes running the components behind a data access page. Because of this, if you try to cancel the event by setting the **ReturnValue** property to **False**, the code will be ignored. However, you can use the DHTML **onbeforeunload** event to display a message box warning the user not to close or navigate away from the page to avoid this.
RecordsetSaveProgress (new)	Occurs repeatedly when the **ExportXML** method is called. Use this event to provide feedback to the user when a recordset is exported.
	This event supports the **ReturnValue** and **PercentComplete** properties of the **DSCEventInfo** object.
	Important At the time this article was written, using the **PercentComplete** property to provide feedback could be somewhat unreliable. Additionally, when running in a Web page, Internet Explorer doesn't update the display of the current page until the script yields control, which won't happen until the **ExportXML** method is finished. As a result, if you add a progress meter to a page that is being saved as XML, it won't appear to update. You can work around this by opening a second window to contain the progress meter, or can create an ActiveX control to listen to the event and display a progress meter.
Undo (new)	Occurs when the user clicks the **Undo** button on the record navigation control, presses the ESC key, or the **Dirty** event is canceled. This event fires before the data is returned to its original values. Use this event to set the conditions under which the user is allowed to undo a change.
	This event supports the **ReturnValue**, **DataPage**, and **Section** properties of the **DSCEventInfo** object.

The Layout of a Data Access Page

The names of the basic parts of a data access page in Design View can be somewhat confusing, so it's important to understand what they refer to and how these parts map to the relevant collections and objects of the Data Source component object model.

The underlying architecture of a data access page varies depending on whether a page utilizes hierarchical grouping. There are two basic kinds of data access pages:

- Simple pages–These pages display fields from a single record at a time with no repeated records or hierarchical grouping. While at run time a simple page has no grouping, in the terms of the underlying data model, it does have a single group level (GroupLevels.Count = 1) and a set of properties associated with that group level. The Employees page in the Northwind Traders sample database is an example of a simple page.

- Banded pages–These pages display multiple records at a time in bands that are repeated down the page. A banded page can either have no hierarchical grouping (essentially a simple page with the DataPageSize property of its single group level set greater than 1), or it can display a hierarchy of related or grouped records. By default, banded pages with grouping display only the first level of hierarchy with lower levels of grouping collapsed beneath expand controls (+ icons). The Review Orders page in the Northwind Traders sample database is an example of a banded page with hierarchical grouping.

The design surface of a data access page can consist of up to four kinds of sections:

- Caption–The first section of a simple page, or the first section of a group level in a banded page, the caption section is most typically used to display column headings for fields displayed in the following header section. However, the caption section can contain any type of control except data-bound controls. When you create a data access page in Design View, the caption section isn't added by default. To add a caption section, right-click a header section, and then click Caption.

- Header–While this section is called the header, it is functionally similar to the detail section of a form or report. The header section is primarily used to display data in data-bound controls and calculated values. A simple page has a single header section that shows one record at a time, whereas a banded page shows multiple records at a time repeating the header section for each record in a grouping level. Banded pages with multiple grouping levels contain nested header sections for each grouping level.

- Footer–The footer section is associated with a header section at the same grouping level. The footer section is typically used to display totals or subtotals for data displayed in the associated header section, although you can also add controls bound to fields and other controls. When you create a data access page in Design View, the footer section isn't added by default. To add a footer section, right-click a header section, and then click Footer. You can't add a footer section to a simple page, or to a banded page that has a single header section. On a page with grouping (pages with a hierarchy of two or more header sections), you can't add a footer section to the lowest (innermost) level in the grouping hierarchy.

- Record Navigation–The record navigation section is the last section of a simple page or a group level in a banded page, and is associated with a header section at the same grouping level. It contains a record navigation control, which is used to move between records, or to add, delete, save, undo changes to, sort, or filter records in the associated header section. The record navigation section can't contain data-bound controls.

Summary

This chapter will briefly covered the Data Source component. In many cases, the Data Source component is used automatically, such as when building a data access page in Design view in Microsoft Access or adding a Chart component to help visualize data stored in a Spreadsheet component. We also introduced the Data Acess page that designed to reproduce many of the features of Microsoft Access forms and reports in Web pages running in Microsoft Internet Explorer 5.0 or later.

For more code sample on Data Access Page, please visit the following web sites:

Creating a Pop-up Data Access Page:
http://msdn.microsoft.com/library/techart/odc_creatingapopup-page.htm

Customizing the Controls on a Data Access Page at Run Time:
http://msdn.microsoft.com/library/techart/odc_customizecon-trols.htm

Embedding an Existing Page in a Data Access Page:
http://msdn.microsoft.com/library/techart/odc_embedpage.htm

Examples of Using Data Access Page Events to Add Custom Functionality:
http://msdn.microsoft.com/library/techart/odc_exampleof-pageevents.htm

Passing Parameters to a Data Access Page:
http://msdn.microsoft.com/library/techart/odc_passparam.htm

Chapter 10

Office XP Web Component Toolpack

Office XP Web Component Toolpack is a valuable toolpack for OWC development. It includes some most up-to-date information and code samples specifically useful for Office XP developers. The size of the set up file is 938,040 bytes. It is available for download from Microsoft's web site since 6/23/2001. You should consider to download the Office XP Web Component Toolpack to your computer if you feel it will be beneficial to you. It is a relatively small file, the download should take less than one minute over standard 56K modem.

Here are some key features for Office XP Web Component Toolpack:

➤ Walkthroughs of new Office XP Web component features

➤ A code sample library of common OWC code snippets

➤ Links to the documentation that comes with Office XP

➤ PivotTable advanced code samples
  —Conditional Cell Coloring via add-in
     (as well as conditional cell coloring via built-in Pivot functionality)
  —Drill through sample

—Actions sample

—Printing via Excel sample

➢ Searchable help files

Figure 10.1 Help files interface

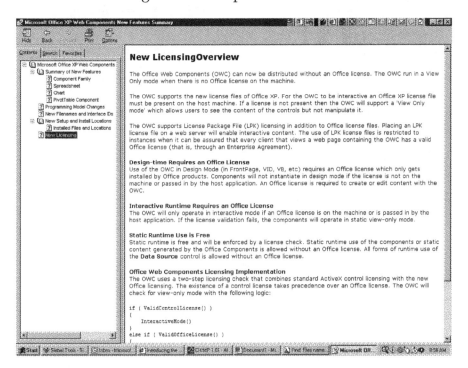

✎ **Note**: Some code samples in the Office XP Web Component Toolpack require a connection to a Microsoft SQL Server 2000 with Analysis Services. SQL Server 2000 must have the FoodMart 2000 sample cube installed.

Download

Currently, the URL for download the Office XP Web Component Toolpack is:

http://msdn.microsoft.com/code/default.asp?url=/msdn-files/026/002/280/Sample%20Files/ExportXML_UseXMLData_htm.asp

Once you are there, click on *download* hyperlink, you will be prompt with the following license agreement dialog box:

Figure 10.2: Office XP Web Component Toolpack License
Agreement Dialog Box

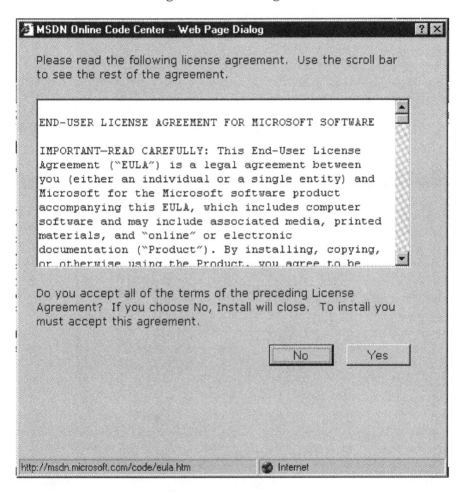

Click on Yes to accept the agreement and you should be able to save
the set up file (offpack.exe) to your local drive.

Installation

Once you have downloaded the Office XP Web Component Toolpack set up executable file. You are ready to install the Office XP Web Component Toolpack on your computer:

> ➢ From the directory you have downloaded the Office XP Web Component Toolpack set up executable file, double click on off-pack.exe file. You should see the following Office XP Web Component Toolpack installation interface:

➤ Click on Next to continue your installation. The default folder
for this Office XP Web Component Toolpack is C:\Program
Files\Office Component Toolpack\.

You can either use this folder or click on Browse to change another
folder:

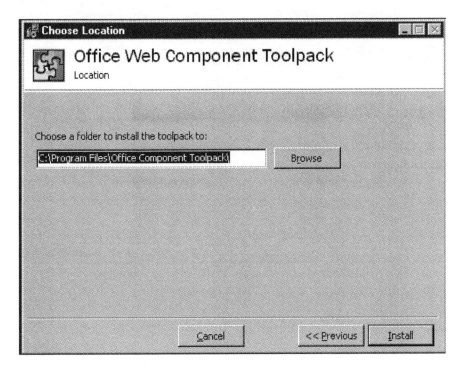

➢ Click on Install to continue the installation process:

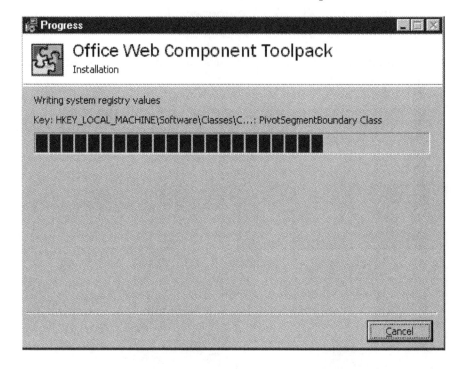

➤ Once the installation process is complete. You should be able to see the confirmation message:

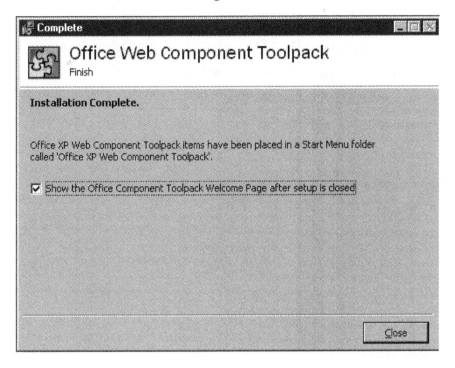

> Click on Close to finish the installation. If you have left the default check box checked for welcome message, you should see the Welcome Interface:

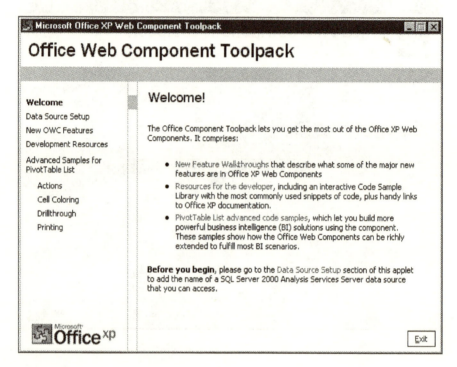

➤ At anytime you want to exit from the application, you can click on Exit button to exit. Before you begin, please go to the Data Source Setup section of this applet to add the name of a SQL Server 2000 Analysis Services Server data source that you can access. You have to set up this connection before you can view code samples. Now you are able to navigate and explore the complete content of Office XP Web Component Toolpack. For example, click on the **New Feature Walkthroughs** will take you to the following interface:

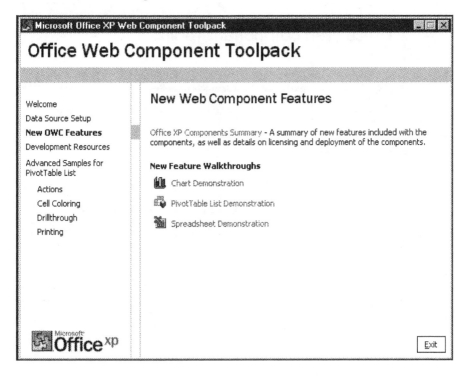

Uninstall or Reinstall

If for any reason you need to uninstall or reinstall the Office XP Web Component Toolpack, you can simply double click on the file off-pack.exe. This executable file will automatically check and see if you have installed the Office XP Web Component Toolpack. If the Office XP Web Component Toolpack has been detected, you will be prompted by the following interface:

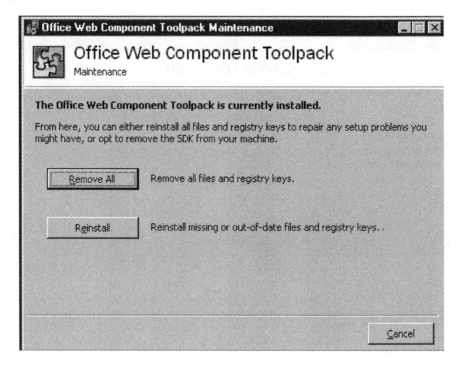

Click on **Remove All** to delete all files and registry keys. Click on **Reinstall** to reinstall missing or out-of-date files and registry keys.

Summary

In this chapter, we covered the basic download, installation, remove, and reinstall process for the Office XP Web Component Toolpack. The Office XP Web Component Toolpack is a great interactive tool for code sample demonstration, programming references and other information.

Appendix A
Active Server Pages Object Model

This appendix details the Active Server Pages Object Model. For each object, there is a description of its properties, methods, and collections.

Request Object

The Request object is used to get information that is sent from the user along with HTTP request. This object along with the Response object, is one of the core objects in the ASP Object Model, and is used extensively when a developer needs to work out what a user wants.

Collections	Description
ClientCertificate	Details the values of client certificates sent from the browser. This is read only.
Cookies	Details the values of any cookies sent in the request from the browser. This is read only.
Form	Used to get data from a submitted form. Values of any elements are read only, and can be accessed by Request.Form("ValueName").value
QueryString	Contains the value of any variables contained in the HTTP string. This is used for sending a request for specific information in a page. Read only.
ServerVariables	Contains values of various HTTP and environment variables on the server. Can provide information such as the server name. Read only.

Property	Description
TotalBytes	This is the number of bytes that the client is sending in the body of the request.

Method	Description
BinaryRead	Used to retrieve data sent to the server from the client as part of the POST request.

Response Object

The Response object is used to control the output from the server to the client. The Response object delivers the feedback based on what the Request object has requested.

Collections	Description
Cookies	This collection is used to specify values of cookies and to send the cookies to the browser.

Properties	Description
Buffer	This indicates whether page output is buffered – meaning it will wait until it is complete before sending it.
CacheControl	Determines whether proxy server can cache the output generated by ASP.
Charset	Appends the name of the character set to the content-type header.
ContentType	Specifies the HTTP content-type of the response – i.e. "Text/HTML".
Expires	Specifies the length of time until a page cached on a browser will expire.
ExpiresAbsolute	Specifies the data and time when a page cached on a browser will expire.
IsClientConnected	Indicates whether the client has disconnected from the server (False), or is still connected (True).

Methods	Description
PICS	This sets the value of the PICS label field in the response header.
Status	Contains the value of the HTTP status line returned by the server.
AddHeader	Adds or changes a value in the HTML header.
AppendToLog	Adds a string to the end of the web server log entry for this request.
BinaryWrite	Send a string to the browser without character set conversion.
Clear	Erases any buffered HTML output.
End	Stops processing the page and immediately returns the current result.
Flush	Sends all buffered output immediately.
Redirect	Sends a redirect message to the browser, instructing it to connect to different URL.
Write	Writes a variable to the current HTTP output as a string.

Application Object

The Application object is used to share information amongst all users of the application. The object stores variables and objects that have an application scope, and information about all currently active sessions within the application.

Collections	Description
Contents	This collection contains all of the items added to the application through script commands.
StaticObjects	This collection contains all of the objects that have been added to the application with the <OBJECT> tag.

Methods	Description
Lock	Locking the application object prevents all other clients from modifying application properties until the Unlock method is called.
Unlock	Allows other clients to modify application properties.
Contents.Remove	Removes a content item from the Contents collection.
Contents.RemoveAll	Removes all contents from the Contents collection.

Events	Description
OnStart	Fires when the first page in the application is referenced.
OnEnd	Fires when the application ends, i.e. when the web server is stopped.

Session Object

The Session object is used to keep track of an individual browser throughout its navigation of your web site. Each browser is given one session, which lasts until the session is terminated, the session times out, or the browser stops navigating the application. The object is used to store information that last for the duration of the session.

Collections	Description
Contents	This collection contains all of the items added to the session through script commands.
StaricObjects	This collection contains all of the objects that have been added to the session with the <OBJECT> tag.

Methods	Description
Abandon	This destroys a Session object and releases its resources on the server.
Contents.Remove	Removes a content item from the Contents collection.
Contents.RemoveAll	Removes all contents from the Contents collection.

Properties	Description
CodePage	Sets the code page that will be used for symbol mapping. A code page is a character set that can include numbers, punctuation marks, and so on.
LCID	Sets the locale identifier, which is a standard international abbreviation that uniquely identifies one of the system-defined locales.
SessionID	Returns the session identification unique to this user.
Timeout	Sets the timeout period, in minutes, for the session state for this application.

Events	Description
OnStart	Fires when the server creates a new session.
OnEnd	Fires when the session is abandoned or time out.

Server Object

The Server object is primarily used to create components that run on the server.

Property	Description
ScriptTimeOut	The length of time that a script can run before an error occurs.

Methods	Description
CreateObject	Creates an instance of an object or server component.
Execute	Executes an .asp file.
GetLastError	Returns an ASPError object that describes the error condition.
HTMLEncode	Applies HEML encoding to the specified string, which replaces certain characters with HTML codes.
MapPath	Converts a virtual path into a physical path.
Transfer	Sends all of the current sat information to another .asp file for processing.
URLEncode	Applices URL encoding, including escape characters, to a string.

ASPError Object

The ASPError object can be used to get information about an error condition that has occurred in an ASP script. The ASPError object is returned by the Server.GetLastError method outlined above. All properties are read only.

Property	Description
ASPCode	This returns an error code as generated by Internet Information Server.
Number	Returns the standard COM error code that has occurred.
Source	Indicates where the error occurred – internal to ASP, in a component, or in a scripting language.
FileName	Indicates the name of the ASP file being processed when the error occurred.
LineNumber	Indicates the line number within the file where the error occurred.
Description	Returns a short description of the error.
ASPDescription	If the error is ASP related, this returns a more detailed description than the Description property.

Appendix B
VB Script Reference

Appendix B covered some VB Script functions and descriptions for your reference since we used VB Script thoughout this book.

Arrays

Dim–declares a variable. An array variable can be static, with a defined number of elements, or dynamic, and can have up to 60 dimensions...

ReDim–used to change the size of an array variable that has been declared as dynamic.

Preserve–used to preserve the contents of an array being resized (otherwise data is lost when ReDim is used). You can only re-dimension the rightmost index of the array.

Erase–reinitializes the elements of a fixed-size array or empties the contents of a dynamic array.

Example:

```
Dim MyStudentArray()
ReDim MyStudentArray(2)

MyStudentArray(2) = "Scott McCoy"

ReDim MyStudentArray(3)
MyStudentArray(3) = "Mary Newman"
```

The contents of MyStudentArray(2) will lost at this point.

```
ReDim Preserve MyStudentArray(5)
MyStudentArray(5) = "David Sobral"
```

The contents of MyStudentArray(3) will be preserved.

```
Erase MyStudentArray
```

All of the contents of MyStudentArray will be erased.

Since all Session-level and Application-level variables are stored as Variants, storing arrays in a Session or Application object is a little bit tricky. To create an array that holds five student names, we need to create the array and then redim it to hold five elements:

```
Dim MyStudentArray()
ReDim MyStudentArray(5)
```

Then we assign each array variable to hold its value respectively:

```
MyStudentArray(0) = "Sam Johnson"
MyStudentArray(5) = "David Sobral"
```

To store the array elements, we have to assign the array into a Session variable:

```
Session("StoredStudentArray") = MyStudentArray
```

To retrieve array elements, we have to use a local array to hold the Session variable's value then access it as normal using indexes:

```
LocalStudentArray = Session("StoredStudentArray")
FirstStudent = LocalStudentArray(1)
```

We can update the array then store it back to the same Session variable:

```
LocalStudentArray(1) = "Joan Hankins"
Session("StoredStudentArray") = LocalStudentArray
```

> **Note**: you can not access an array like this:
>
> ```
> FirstStudent = Session("StoredStudentArray")(1)
> ```
>
> This is not going to work and will cause data loss.

LBound–returns the smallest subscript for the dimension of an array. Note that arrays always start from the subscript zero so this function will always return the values zero.

UBound–used to determine the size of an array.

```
Dim MyStudentArray(8,5)
```

The following code will returns 8 for the first array dimension:

```
intFirstDimensionSize = UBound (MyStudentArray, 1)
```

The following code will returns 5 for the first array dimension:

```
intFirstDimensionSize = UBound (MyStudentArray, 2)
```

Since the arrays starts from zero, the actual number of elements is always one greater than the value returned by the UBound function.

Assignments

Let–used to assign values to variables (optional).
Set–used to assign an object reference to a variable.

```
Let intNumStudents = 34

Set txtSchoolName = txtControl
txtSchoolName.value = "Edison High School"
```

Constants

Empty–an empty variable is one that has been create, but has not yet been assigned a value.

Nothing–used to remove an object reference.

```
Set txtSchoolName = txtControl
Set txtSchoolName = Nothing
```

Null–indicates that a variable is not valid. Note that this isn't the same as Empty.

True–indicates that an expression is true. Has numerical value–1.

False–indicates that an expressionis false. Has numerical value 0.

Error Constant

Constant	Value
vbObjectError	&h80040000

System Color Constants

Constant	Value	Description
vbBlack	&h000000	Black
vbRed	&hFF0000	Red
vbGreen	&h00FF00	Green
vbYellow	&hFFFF00	Yellow
vbBlue	&hooooFF	Blue
vbMagenta	&hFF00FF	Magenta
vbCyan	&h00FFFF	Cyan
vbWhite	&hFFFFFF	White

Comparison Constants

Constant	Value	Description
vbBinarCompare	0	Perform a binary comparison
vbTextCompare	1	Perform a textual comparison

Date and Time Constants

Constant	Value	Description
vbSunday	1	Sunday
vbMonday	2	Monday
vbTuesday	3	Tuesday
vbWednesday	4	Wednesday
vbThursday	5	Thursday
vbFriday	6	Friday
vbSaturday	7	Saturday
vbFirstJan1	1	Use the week in which January 1 occurs (default).
vbFirstFourDays	2	Use the first week that has at least four days in the new year.
vbFistFullWeek	3	Use the first full week of the year.
vbUseSystem	0	Use the format in the regional settings for the computer.
vbUseSystemDayOfWeek	0	Use the day in the system settings for the first weekday.

Date Format Constants

Constant	Value	Description
vbGeneralDate	0	Display a date and /or time in the format set in the system settings. For real numbers display only a date. For numbers less than 1, display time only.
vbLongDate	1	Display a date using the long date format specified in the computer's regional settings.
vbShortDate	2	Display a date using the short date format specified in the computer's regional settings.
vbLongTime	3	Display a time using the long time format specified in the computer's regional settings.
vbShortTime	4	Display a time using the short time format specified in the computer's regional settings.

Message Box Constants

Constant	Value	Description
vbOkOnly	0	Display OK button only.
vbOKCancel	1	Display OK and Cancel buttons.
vbAbortRetryIgnore	2	Display Abort, Retry, and Ignore buttons.
vbYesNoCancel	3	Display Yes, No, and Cancel buttons.
vbYesNo	4	Display Yes and No buttons.
vbRetryCancel	5	Display Retry and Cancel buttons.
vbCritical	16	Display Critical Message icon.
vbQuestion	32	Display Warning Query icon.
vbExclamation	48	Display Warning Message icon.
vbInfomration	64	Display Information Message icon.
vbDefaultButton1	0	First button is the default.
vbDefaultButton2	256	Second button is the default.
vbDefaultButton3	512	Third button is the default.
vbDefaultButton4	768	Fourth button is the default.
vbApplicationModal	0	Application modal.
vbSystemModal	4096	System modal.

String Constants

Constant	Value	Description
vbCr	Chr(13)	Carriage return only.
vbCrLf	Chr(13) & Chr (10)	Carriage return and linefeed (Newline).
vbFormFeed	Chr(12)	Form feed only.
vbLf	Chr (10)	Line feed only.
vbNewLine	-	Newline character as appropriate to a specific platform.
vbNullChar	Chr(0)	Character having the value 0.
vbNullString	-	String having the value zero (not just an empty string).
vbTab	Chr(9)	Horizontal tab.
vbVerticalTab	Chr(11)	Vertical tab.

Tristate Constants

Constant	Value	Description
TristateUseDefault	-2	Use default setting
TristateTrue	-1	True
TristateFalse	0	False

VarType Constants

Constant	Value	Description
vbEmpty	0	Uninitialized
vbNull	1	Contains no valid data
vbInteger	2	Integer subtype
vbLong	3	Long subtype
vbSingle	4	Single subtype
vbDouble	5	Double subtype
vbCurrency	6	Currency subtype
vbDate	7	Date subtype
vbString	8	String subtype
vbObject	9	Object
vbError	10	Error subtype
vbBoolean	11	Boolean subtype
vbVariant	12	Variant (used only for arrays of variants)
vbDataObject	13	Data access object
vbDecimal	14	Decimal subtype
vbByte	17	Byte subtype.
vbArray	8192	Array

Functions

Conversion Functions

Function	Description
Abs	Returns the absolute value of a number.
Asc	Returns the numeric ANSI (or ASCII) code number of the first character in a string.
AscB	As above, but provide for use with byte data contained in a string. Returns result from the first byte only.
AscW	As above, but provided for Unicode characters. Returns the Wide character code, avoiding the conversion from Unicode to ANSI.
Chr	Returns a string made up of the ANSI character matching the number supplied.
ChrB	As above, but provided for use with byte data contained in a string. Always returns a sinle byte.
ChrW	As above, but provide for Unicode characters. Its argument is a Wide character code, therby avoiding the conversion from ANSI to Unicode.
CBool	Returns the argument value converted to a Variant of subtype Boolean.
Cbyte	Returns the argument value converted to a Variant of subtype Bte.
CCur	Returns the argument value converted to a Variant of subtype Currency.
CDate	Returns the argument value converted to a Variant of subtype Date.
CDbl	Returns the argument value converted to a Variant of subtype Double.
CInt	Returns the argument value converted to a Variant of subtype Integer.

CLng	Returns the argument value converted to a Variant of subtype Long
CSng	Returns the argument value converted to a Variant of subtype Single
Fix	Returns the integer (whole) part of a number. If the number is negative, Fix returns the first negative integer greater than or equal to the number.
Hex	Returns a string representing the hexadecimal value of a number.
Int	Int returns the first negative integer less than or equal to the number.
Oct	Retuns a string representing the octal value of a number.
Round	Returns a number rounded to a specified number of decimal places.
Sgn	Reutrns an integer indicating the sign of a number.

Date/Time Functions

Function	Description
Date	Returns the current system date.
DateAdd	Returns a date to which a specified time interval has been added.
DateDiff	Returns the number of days, weeks, or years between two dates.
DatePart	Returns just the day, month or year of a given date.
DateSerial	Returns a Variant of subtype Date for a specified year, month and day.
DateValue	Returns a Variant of subtype Date.
Day	Returns a number between 1 and 31 representing the day of the month.
Hour	Returns a number between 0 and 23 representing the house of the day.
Minute	Returns a number between 0 and 59 representing the minute of the hour.
Month	Returns a number between 1 and 12 representing the month of the year.
MonthName	Returns the name of the specified month as a string.
Now	Returns the current date and time.
Second	Returns a number between 0 and 59 representing the second of the minute.
Time	Returns a Variant of subtype Date indicting the current system time.
TimeSerial	Returns a Variant of subtype Date for a specified hour, minute, and second.
TimeValue	Returns a Variant of subtype date containing the time.
Weekday	Returns a number representing the day of the week.
WeekdayName	Returns the name of the specified day of the week as a string.
Year	Returns the number representing the eyar.

Math Functions

Function	Description
Atn	Returns the arctangent of a number.
Cos	Returns the cosine of an angle.
Exp	Returns e (the base of natural logarithms) raised to a power.
Log	Returns the natural logarithm of a number.
Randomize	Initilazes the random-number generator.
Rnd	Returns a random number.
Siin	Returns the sine of an angle.
Sqr	Returns the square root of a number
Tan	Reutns the tangent of an angle.

Miscellaneous Functions

Function	Description
Eval	Evaluates an expression and returns a Boolean result (e.g. treats x=y as an expression which is either true or false).
Execute	Execute one or more statements (e.g. treats x=y as a statement which assigns the value of y to x).
RGB	Returns a number representing an RGB color value.

Index

D

E

F

www.ingramcontent.com/pod-product-compliance
Lightning Source LLC
Chambersburg PA
CBHW051223050326
40689CB00007B/782